PALLADIO

ANDREAS PALLADIVS

ex eleganti antiqua tabella
apud March.ᵐ Marium Capra Patricium Vicentinum

PALLADIO

A Western Progress

Desmond Guinness and Julius Trousdale Sadler, Jr.

A Studio Book   THE VIKING PRESS   New York

By the same authors
Mr. Jefferson, Architect

Library of Congress Cataloging in Publication Data

Guinness, Desmond.
  Palladio: a western progress.
  (A Studio book)
  Bibliography: p.
  Includes index.
  1. Palladio, Andrea, 1508–1580. 2. Neoclassi-
cism (Architecture)—Italy. 3. Neoclassicism (Archi-
tecture)—England. 4. Neoclassicism (Architecture)
—Ireland. 5. Neoclassicism (Architecture)—United
States. 6. Neoclassicism (Architecture)—West In-
dies.
I. Sadler, Julius Trousdale, joint author. II. Title.
NA1123.P2G78   724′.1   75–38760
ISBN 0–670–53732–2

◄ Andrea Palladio: engraving from a book on the churches of Vicenza by Enea Arnaldi, published in 1767.

Acknowledgments

The authors wish to express their thanks for the kindness, cooperation, and hospitality extended to them by the owners or occupants of the houses which appear in this book: Captain and Mrs. Richard K. Anderson, Prince and Princess Biondi Morra, His Grace the Duke of Beaufort, Mr. and Mrs. William B. Beverley, Mrs. William N. Beverley, Mr. and Mrs. Claus Von Bülow, Mr. and Mrs. Hill Carter, Representative and Mrs. Robert W. Daniel, Jr., Mr. and Mrs. Joseph F. Johnston, The Earl of Leicester, Mr. and Mrs. Edward Manigault, Delegate and Mrs. Lewis A. M. McMurran, Jr., Sir Oswald and Lady Mosley, Lord and Lady Moyne, The Hon. David and Mrs. Nall–Cain, Mr. and Mrs. John H. G. Pell, Mr. and Mrs. Russell Perkinson, Mr. and and Mrs. Richard H. Rush, Mr. and Mrs. Charles Scarlett, Jr., Mrs. Morgan B. Schiller, Miss Rosanna Seaborn, Mr. and Mrs. Parker Snead, Mr. Chauncey D. Stillman, Colonel and Mrs. Henry Gwynne Tayloe, and Mr. and Mrs. Ronald Tree.

We are equally obliged to those who gave their invaluable assistance in the compilation of research, among them: James Baxter Bailey, Charles N. Bayless, Marcus Binney, Bennie Brown, Jr., Paul Buchanan, Miss Gertrude Carraway, Mrs. Joseph Carson, John Castellani, Professor Renato Cevese, Clement Conger, John Cornforth, Dewey Lee Curtis, Penelope Cuthbertson, Virginia Daiker, Mrs. S. Henry Edmunds, John Page Elliott, Susan H. Ewell, the Knight of Glin, Mrs. Alan Hale, John Harris, Richard H. Jenrette, Gregory Johnson, Douglas Lewis, Robert F. Looney, Christine Meadows, John F. Miller, Herbert Mitchell, David Nathans, Maria Vittoria Pellizzari, Adolf Placzek, Mrs. Wayne Plunkett, Virginia Radcliffe, Mrs. J. P. Robinson, Jr., Raymond Shepherd, and James Waite.

We are, of course, especially indebted to the kindly folk on both sides of the water who provided us with hospitality, history, and good cheer on our wanderings: Mr. and Mrs. Thomas Berry, Lady Cusack–Smith, Mr. and the Hon. Mrs. Peter Gill, Mr. and Mrs. George E. Lane–Fox, Mr. and Mrs. Thomas Lefevre, Mr. and Mrs. James E. Lewis, Dr. and Mrs. E. D. Vere Nicoll, Mr. and Mrs. James C. Rea, Jr., Mr. and Mrs. Edward Richardson, Mr. and Mrs. William Ryan, and Mr. and Mrs. James Watts.

Finally, the authors wish to acknowledge their gratitude to Mary Velthoven for her patience, persistence, accuracy, and equanimity.

This book is dedicated to
Marina Luling,
first member of the Irish Georgian Society,
and
Jacquelin D. J. Sadler

CONTENTS

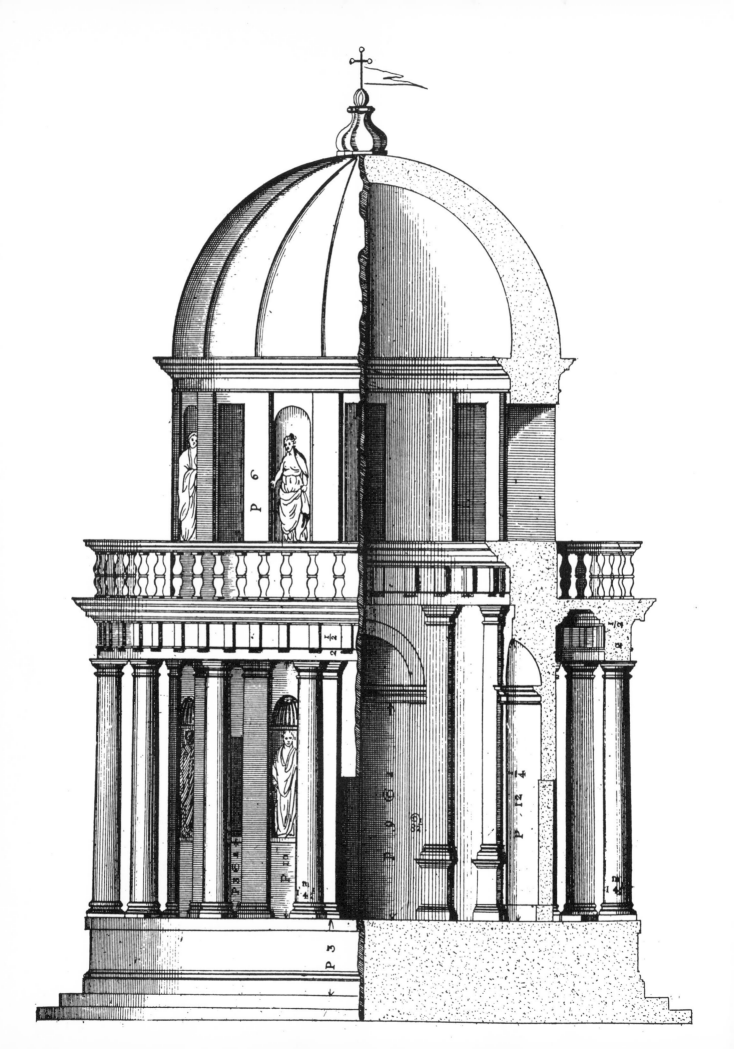

"it seemed to me a thing worthy of a man, who ought not to be born for himself only, but also for the utility of others, to publish the designs of those edifices, (in collecting which, I have employed so much time, and exposed myself to so many dangers) . . . ."

—Palladio, I Quattro Libri dell' Architettura,
Venice, 1570

ITALY

Andrea Palladio is the only architect whose name has been immortalized in a style of building known throughout the world. The influence of his architecture is to be found amid the snows of Russia, under the relentless Indian sun, and as far afield as Australia and America. The Palladian style reigned supreme in Colonial America. Free to develop in an architectural void, it remained the accepted style of building for a hundred years until the Greek and Gothic Revivals of the 1830s and the Victorian revolt which followed. Indeed the light was never quite extinguished; in parts of the New World Palladianism even now continues to flourish. Simple lines and satisfying proportions have an enduring quality above the dictates of fashion.

Palladio was one of many architects who, from the time of the Renaissance, looked to classical antiquity for inspiration. He is remembered at the expense of his contemporaries largely because he published his designs. His mission was to "free" his country from the Gothic in a return to "correct" classical proportions and a proper understanding of the orders. These he explained and illustrated in *I Quattro Libri dell' Architettura*, which first appeared in 1570, and Palladio sums up the work in the preface (taken from Ware's edition, 1738):

> The first part shall be divided into two books; in the first shall be treated of the preparation of the materials, and when prepared, how, and in what manner, they ought to be put to use, from the foundation up to the roof: where those precepts shall be, that are universal, and ought to be observed in all edifices, as well private as publick.

> In the second I shall treat of the quality of the fabricks that are suitable to the different ranks of men: first of those of a city; and then of the most convenient situation for villa's, and in what manner they are to be disposed.

". . . the elevation of both the outside and in" of Bramante's S. Pietro Martirio from Book 4, Plate XLV of the *Quattro Libri*.

9

The Villa Maser, Treviso, built by Palladio c. 1560 for the Barbaro family.

Detail of the pediment of the villa.

The nymphaeum behind the Villa Maser forms a secret garden, peopled with lively statues of classical deities by Alessandro Vittoria.

Detail of the nymphaeum.

And as we have but very few examples from the antients, of which we can make use, I shall insert the plans and elevations of many fabricks I have erected, for different gentlemen, . . .

The *Quattro Libri* describe and illustrate the various types and combinations of orders that constitute "correct" architecture. Palladio's theories on town houses and country villas are explained, and most of his architectural invention to date, with the exception of the Venetian churches, is illustrated in the first three books. Book IV contains the "Antient Temples" of Rome, which Palladio had drawn and measured with his own hand.

These volumes enjoyed an immediate success, ran into many editions, and were translated into every major European language. As a result, Palladio was established as pre-eminent among the architects of his time, and he has been regarded ever since as the instigator of the movement for a return to classicism.

The Palladian style was summed up by Sir William Chambers in his *Treatise on Civil Architecture* (1759): "Amongst the restorers of the ancient Roman architecture, the style of Palladio is correct and elegant, his general dispositions are often happy, his outlines distinct and regular, his forms graceful; little appears that could with propriety be spared, nothing seems wanting, and all his measures accord so well that no part attracts the attention in prejudice to any of the rest." Regular—elegant—happy; by no means all his buildings can be so described. The Villa Sarego at Santa Sofia, Verona, has, in Palladio's own words, "a courtyard surrounded by porticos; here the columns are in Ionic style and made of rough stone; in fact this is what country life should tend to, as here simple and genuine things seem more proper than refined ones." The columns are oppressive and crude, and appear to have been made of ill-assorted millstones. This was not a design that appealed to his imitators. Palladio was an imaginative and creative artist, not afraid to experiment or to borrow ideas from others. The plainness that appealed to the puritan spirit is not invariably found in his buildings. The outside walls of the Palazzo Barbarano and the Capitaniato Loggia in Vicenza are heavily encrusted with plaster decoration. His buildings are considered tranquil and serene, but the Palazzo Thiene frowns across its narrow Vicenza street as disapprovingly as any Florentine palace of the time. Chambers's analysis of Palladio is consistent with the accepted opinion of his work even today. His innovative talents and his passion for experiment, although not always successful, deserve to be remembered also.

> There is a tide in the affairs of men,
> Which, taken at the flood, leads on to fortune; . . .

The Great Fire of London gave Wren his opening, chance brought Gandon to Dublin rather than St. Petersburg, and fate was also kind to Palladio. He was born at a place and time that offered great opportunities, for both political and social reasons. Little is known of his life. Andrea di Pietro dalla Gondola was born in Padua of humble parentage in 1508. He was apprenticed at an early age to a stonecutter, but broke his bond when he was sixteen and went to Vicenza. There he worked for the next fourteen years under two sculptors named Porlezza and Pittoni. At the age of thirty he was taken up by Count Giangiorgio Trissino, whose house was a meeting place for artists and learned men. Trissino was a true product of the Renaissance; poet, philosopher, musician, he also took a great interest in the visual arts. He wrote an epic poem entitled *Italy Liberated from the Goths*, in which there is a winged messenger called Palladio, and the name was adopted by the young architect.

Palladio and Trissino visited Rome together in 1541 and 1545, when a prolonged stay allowed time for drawing and measuring the ancient remains of the city. Palladio published the results of this work in 1554 in a small book entitled *L'Antichita di Roma*. Trissino died in 1550. Private patronage can seldom have had more far-reaching results. By the time of his patron's death, Palladio was established as an architect, with several buildings to his credit. He lived and worked

Giustiniana Giustiniani, the wife of Marcantonio Barbaro, with her nurse in Paolo Veronese's fresco, c. 1561.

Paolo Veronese's frescoes in the Villa Maser intermingle classical allegories with scenes of the Veneto. It is generally agreed that his brother Benedetto was responsible for the architectural framework.

The entire piano nobile is frescoed. The rooms below were the offices of a working farm.

The *Tempietto* at the foot of the villa's garden was completed in 1580, the year Palladio died.

in and around Vicenza until 1570 when, following the loss of his two sons, he moved to Venice. He died in 1580 and is buried in Vicenza beneath an elaborate memorial by Canova, erected in 1845.

The Veneto, of which Vicenza is one of the principal cities, is that part of the Italian mainland closest to Venice. A Venetian governor was appointed to Vicenza by the Doge every two years. The local aristocracy, however, looked not to Venice but to the Holy Roman Empire for their titles; known as the *nobiltà della terra*, they were somewhat looked down on by the Venetians. It was of paramount importance to Venice that her wealth be concentrated in the merchant shipping which was the very lifeblood of the city-state, and the aristocracy had always been discouraged from buying land and dissipating this wealth in the building of country houses.

By 1530 the Venetians had lost their stranglehold on European trade with the East. Their ships were cumbersome and outmoded. They were at the mercy of fluctuating grain prices, which were at times inflationary, and the authorities were forced to turn their attention inland. They offered

The interior of the *Tempietto*.

S. Giorgio Maggiore (1565): the earliest of Palladio's four Venetian churches.

The Villa Rotonda, Vicenza, was built by Palladio c. 1567 as a belvedere for musical entertainment.

An overdoor contains the painting of a bearded man, thought to be Palladio, pointing toward a building resembling the villa.

The central hall of the Rotonda with its frescoed dome was open to the sky for a hundred years.

grants to meet the cost of reclaiming the swampy marshland and rendering it fruitful, waterways were dredged for transport, and modern farming methods began to replace the old feudal customs.

Palladio appeared on the scene at this propitious moment. Although he was not trained as an architect, his original apprenticeship and his long years in the sculptors' studio had made him familiar with the mysteries of carving and stonecutting. He had a powerful patron in Trissino. Above all, he had the genius and ambition necessary to achieve a spectacular career, echoes of which were to travel the world.

Elevation and plan of the Rotonda from the *Quattro Libri.*

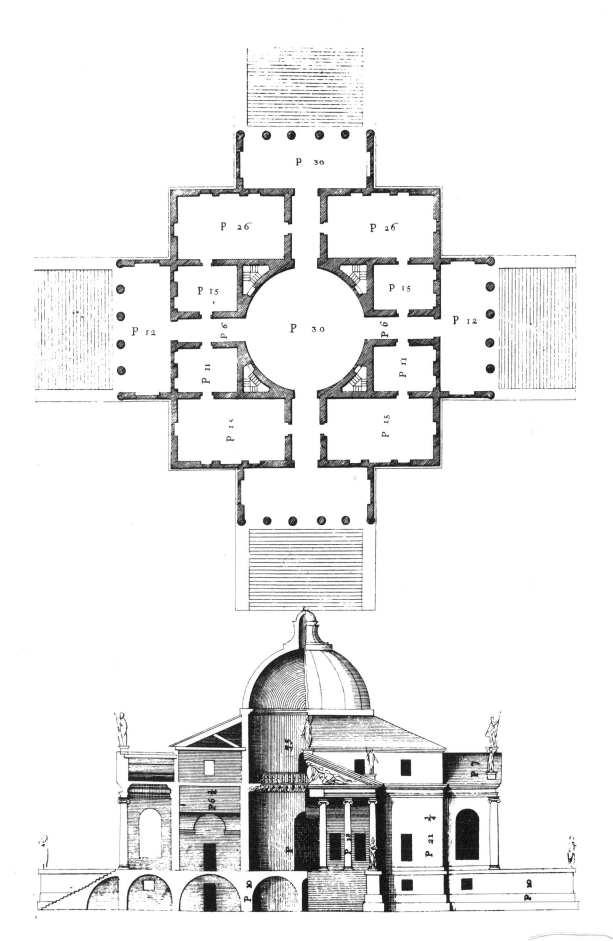

P 30

P 26   P 26

P 15   P 15

P 12   P 6   P 6   P 12

P 30

P 11   P 11

P 15   P 15

The Villa Malcontenta, built by Palladio c. 1555 on the banks of the Brenta.

The Villa Maser was built in 1560 by Palladio for two brothers, Daniele and Marcantonio Barbaro. Daniele was Patriarch of Aquileja, and as the editor of Vitruvius, the Augustan Age theorist and author, he must have had ideas on architecture in sympathy with those of Palladio. Marcantonio was a sometime ambassador of the Venetian Republic to France and Turkey. His wife, Giustiniana Giustiniani, is depicted in fresco in the "Hall of Olympus" leaning over the balcony to receive her guests, her pet dog perched on the balustrade, and an old nurse at her side.

The villa stands proudly on a gentle slope, like a great yellow bird with wings outstretched, about to fly across the broad, fertile plain beneath. Behind, a semicircular screen forms a little private court or *nymphaeum*, with a pond in which is reflected an array of grotesque statues by Vittoria, the stuccoist and sculptor. Palladio was punctilious in recording the names of those who decorated the interiors of his buildings, and it is strange that he makes no mention of Veronese's work here. It is the great beauty of Maser. Every room on the piano nobile is coved, and frescoed with amazing virtuosity. The effect is breathtaking, and the architect may have felt that his contribution took second place. Veronese's flights of fancy are framed by painted columns and cornices; landscapes, seen through imaginary openings, are peopled with fantastic buildings and ruins.

The vast cruciform hall of the Malcontenta with its faded frescoes by G. B. Zelotti.

This elaborate decoration is on one plane; below, to either side of the central block, are the rooms for making and storing wine, the dairy, and so on, that were once part of the farm.

At the foot of the garden stands the *Tempietto*, a little family church designed by Palladio some twenty years after the villa was built. The Latin frieze gives the date as 1580, the year of its completion and of the architect's death. A sketch by Palladio of the "Temple of Romulus," now at the Royal Institute of British Architects, provided the inspiration for the *Tempietto* at Maser, which is built in the form of a Greek cross within a circle. The human scale and intimate proportions of the *Tempietto* can be seen in the illustration on page 14. It was not put up in time to be included in the *Quattro Libri*, and was rather off the customary route taken by eighteenth-century travelers; otherwise its example would surely have been followed elsewhere. Palladio was able to provide the Barbaro family with the temple church he wanted to build in Venice, where he was subject to the prejudices of a conservative clergy and the practical needs of a populous city.

Palladio's ecclesiastical commissions are variations on the temple theme, as might be expected from one immersed in the buildings of ancient Rome. Whereas his villas are of brick or

The Villa Badoer (1554), Fratta Polesine, is the only existing example of a villa by Palladio with curved sweeps. It contains frescoes by Giallo Fiorentino.

Villa Saraceno (1560), Finale di Agugliaro, is the smallest and one of the most exquisite examples of Palladio's work.

rubble stuccoed, the Venetian churches are built of more lasting materials, faced in the pure white stone called *pietro d'Istria*. His best-known churches are the Redentore (1576) and S. Giorgio Maggiore (1565), which dominates Venice from its island retreat, the changing light adding drama to its simple lines. The double pediment found on all Palladio's Venetian churches was his own invention. It serves to bring together the whole front of the building into one unified façade and is practical in that the lower pediment conceals the falling roofline to either side. It was borrowed by Kent for his temple at Holkham in Norfolk, can be seen fronting the temple at Castle Ward in Ireland, and also found its way to the Redwood Library at Newport, Rhode Island.

The Villa Capra, or Rotonda, surmounts a small hill a mile from Vicenza. From the four porticoes the view of the countryside may be enjoyed in every direction. It was built in 1567 for Paolo Almerico, who died in 1589. In 1591 it was bought by the Counts Capra, whose name is writ bold beneath the pediment; the family died out in the last century. In 1912 it was acquired by Count Andrea di Valmarana, the present owner. When Inigo Jones visited the Rotonda at the beginning of the seventeenth century, there was no glass covering on the center of the dome, which was open to the sky apart from "a net to keep out the Flyes." It was built for entertaining on warm summer evenings, when music was played by moonlight in the great rotunda beneath the painted dome.

Four variations on this theme were built in England, and Thomas Jefferson's entry for the President's Palace competition in 1792, had it been selected, would have given one to the New

The entrance hall of the Villa Cornaro.

Villa Cornaro (1554), Piombino Dese. Palladio's double portico was much imitated in Colonial America.

World. With the Malcontenta it is the best known of all the Palladian villas, and despite its proximity to Vicenza, the most dramatically situated.

La Malcontenta (c. 1555), the villa Palladio built for the Foscari, which once again belongs to that family, sits dreaming by the banks of the Brenta on the outskirts of Venice. Within, a vast cruciform central space is adorned with faded frescoes, ghosts of their former selves, emphasizing the gentle melancholy of the villa shrouded from the world behind its curtain of weeping willows. Although Malcontenta was much admired by travelers on their way to Venice, it was Badoer, despite its comparative remoteness, that had the greatest influence abroad.

The Villa Badoer (1554) at Fratta Polesine was a working farm as well as a country retreat. It is not without reason that the curved and colonnaded *barchesse* stretch forward in a gesture of eternal welcome. Such an arrangement made the supervision of the estate easier, and Palladio himself gives specific advice on the practical organization of the farm buildings to this end. "The grange, where the corn is threshed, ought to be exposed to the sun, ample, spacious, paved, and a little raised in the middle, with portico's round it, or at least on one side; that in case of sudden rains, the corn may be immediately conveyed under cover; and must not be too near the master's house, by reason of the dust, nor so far off as to be *out of sight.*" [Authors' italics.] The grange was to be in view so that the owner could keep a watchful eye on the business of the farm. It is hard to believe that this would have applied in the palatial splendors of a Maser or a Malcontenta. Badoer is an agricultural complex, of a kind imitated wherever Palladio's influence is found. The "economic Palladian layout," combining elegance with practicality, was born here.

The Villa Saraceno (1560) is even more modest in scale than Badoer. Beneath a simple pediment, three arches, raised above the level of the flanking colonade, form the entrance loggia with its frescoed ceiling. To either side, one pedimented window; *sonst nichts.* Line and shadow are the cheapest form of ornament, and Saraceno is as pure an expression of the Palladian idiom as there is.

The Villa Cornaro stands well back from the street of the small town of Piombino Dese, with a large garden behind. It has the serene air of a country villa, and being of stucco rather than

A drawing of 1613 of the Villa Cornaro found in the Museo Civico Correr, Venice, by Douglas Lewis.

Villa Piovene, Lonedo. From a mural by James Reynolds, commissioned by Mr. and Mrs. Thomas W. Berry. The villa was built by Palladio c. 1538; the portico, also to his design, was added after his death. The great Francesco Muttoni staircase dates from the early eighteenth century. Villa Piovene looks toward the Villa Godi (c. 1537), Palladio's first commission, which stands a little way down the hill.

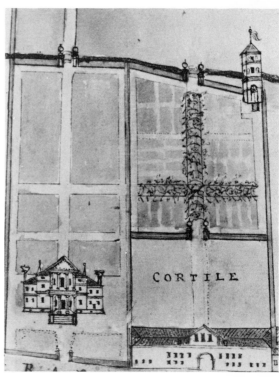

The Palazzo Thiene, Vicenza, in a drawing by one of Sir John Soane's draftsmen.

stone is quite distinct from Palladio's town houses. The interior has frescoes by Mattia Bortoloni, painted in 1717, as well as mantels and plaster decoration of this later period. The building was completed in 1554, when the gardens were laid out as shown in the accompanying drawing of 1613, which was rediscovered by Douglas Lewis in 1971 and first published in the *Bollettino del Centro Internazionale di Studi di Architettura Andrea Palladio* in 1972.

Palladio prepared a scheme for a bridge in Venice with shops on it, which is published in Book III of the *Quattro Libri*, Chapter XIII. This was rejected in favor of a design by Sansovino that itself was not carried out, because of the Turkish war. The Rialto bridge was erected in 1588 to the plans (suitably enough) of Antonio da Ponte. Palladio's design was more theatrical although less Venetian than the one chosen. It is best seen in the accompanying *Capriccio* of Palladian buildings by Canaletto, standing between the Palazzo Chiericati and the Basilica, which Canaletto transported from Vicenza to Venice in his imagination. Palladio does not specify that his design relates to the Rialto project, but declares that it is "in the middle of a city, that is one of the greatest, and [one] of the most noble in *Italy*, and is the metropolis of many other cities." There were to be no less than six rows of shops and three streets over the Grand Canal, as well as loggias "in which the merchants might have assembled to negotiate together."

In the last year of his life Palladio designed the Teatro Olimpico in Vicenza. His theatre is built of wood and has an elaborate architectural backdrop with perspectives seen through three openings. It is still in use today, candlelit for concerts, with the fire engine standing by. The beauty of the interior compensates for the fact that in imitation of the true amphitheatre the seats are bare boards.

The handful of Palladian buildings shown here are representative of his most influential work. There is no typical Palladian villa; he was too inventive an architect for that, and his designs show considerable variety. It was left to his followers, both in the Veneto and beyond the Alps, to identify his name with buildings of temple form.

An imaginative painting by Canaletto of Palladio's rejected design for the Rialto bridge in Venice. To the left, the Palazzo Chiericati (1550); at the right, the Basilica (1549). Both by Palladio, the buildings are in fact at Vicenza.

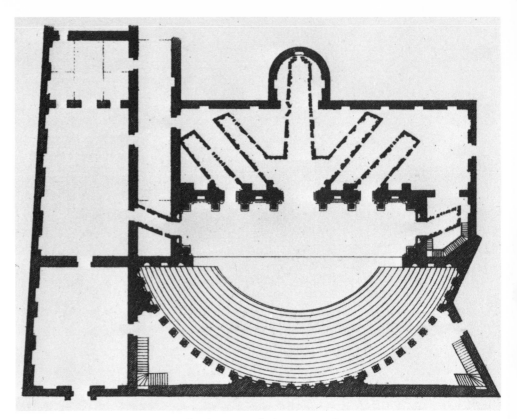

A plan of the theatre, with the stage at the top.

A wooden model made by Palladio of the Teatro Olimpico (1580), Vicenza, now in the Boston Athenaeum, showing the exterior, which was not completed.

Teatro Olimpico: the proscenium, with perspective backdrop.

OVERLEAF: The amphitheatre of the Teatro Olimpico.

A late flowering of the Palladian style in France, the Temple de la Gloire (1800) in Orsay was built by Vignon, architect of the Madeleine, for one of Napoleon's generals.

*"A new architectural religion was born, with Palladio
as Mahomet, his Four Books of Architecture as the sacred
text, and Inigo Jones as a major prophet. Of the new
cult Lord Burlington was to be the high priest and
Chiswick the temple."*

—*John Charlton*

ENGLAND

Palladio's influence traveled northward through England and Ireland to America without linger-
ing on the Continent. Le Vau, Gabriel, and their followers were, of course, imbued with the
classical spirit, but it was with the Empire that simple lines, inspired by Egypt and Greece, came
into their own.

It was to the puritan spirit that the economy of ornament in Palladio's chaste, understated
buildings appealed. Apart from Ireland, the countries that came under his spell were Protestant
nations where the baroque meant Rome, incense, and the graven image. In Ireland a Protestant
oligarchy ruled the country, and although the majority of the people had clung to the old faith, the
Penal Laws kept them from positions of influence, and they had little say in the architectural
achievements of the period.

Inigo Jones (1573–1652), who visited the Palladian villas in 1614, *Quattro Libri* in hand
(his copy, copiously annotated, is now at Worcester College, Oxford), was the first to introduce
the style to England. Rudolph Wittkower, in his book, *Palladio and English Palladianism*, has
shown, through an illuminating contemporary description of Jones by the Papal agent at the Court
of James I, that the architect, although born a Catholic, was a proud and determined puritan. His
taste in architecture, as Summerson has noted, is summed up in his own words, written in an
Italian sketchbook in 1615:

> And to saie trew all thes composed ornaments the wch Proceed out of y^e
> aboundance of dessigners and wear brought in by Michill Angell and his followers in
> my opignion do not well in sollid Architecture and ye fasciati of houses, but in gardens
> loggis stucco or ornaments of chimnies peeces or in the inner parts of houses thos com-
> positiones are of necessety to be yoused. For as outwarly every wyse mā carrieth a graviti
> in Publicke Places, whear ther is nothing els looked for, yet inwardly hath his im-
> maginacy set on fire, and sumtimes licenciously flying out, as nature hir sealf doeth often

The earliest Palladian building in England is the Queen's House, Greenwich, built in 1616 by Inigo Jones.

tymes stravagantly, to dellight, amase us sumtimes moufe us to laughter, sumtimes to contemplation and horror, so in architecture ye outward ornaments oft [ought] to be sollid, proporsionable according to the rulles, masculine and unaffected.

Inigo Jones was appointed Surveyor of the King's Works in 1615 and began work on the Queen's House, Greenwich, in the following year. Its unaffected design owes much to Palladian example. It was, however, as remote from the taste of the country as a whole as the jokes of the Court from those of the tavern. It was a building designed by a courtier for his Queen, and the rest of the country, if it gave a thought to architectural matters, would have reckoned it odd and insipid in its stark modernity. Jones was years ahead of his time. Hardwicke Hall, in all its ungainly splendor, is but twenty years older; the Queen's House was built hard on the heels of the Elizabethan prodigy houses.

The Queen's House is designed to form a bridge over what was once the public road from Deptford to Woolwich, so that its occupants might enjoy complete privacy and watch the comings and goings below if they felt inclined. It is symmetrical; the entrance hall is on axis to the front door, so different from the Tudor convention where the entrance was often at one end, separated from the main body of the great hall by a carved screen. The hall is a forty-foot cube, with a compartmented ceiling and a cantilevered gallery surrounding it at the upper level. There are echoes of the Rotonda here, and a hundred years later Colen Campbell borrowed the design for the Stone Hall at Houghton. The Queen's House is approached from the river, and today the Italianate loggia looks out over the deer park to the domes and cupolas of the Royal Observatory. If there is a flaw in the design it is that the central arched window of the entrance front is not strong enough to dominate the façade, underlining a lateral emphasis also found in the Banqueting House.

The street elevation of the Banqueting House on Whitehall has likewise no central motif, and the emphasis is horizontal rather than vertical. Inigo Jones had been a designer of masques at the Court of James I, and it was fitting that the Banqueting House should be opened in 1622 with Ben Jonson's *Masque of Augurs*. When the great painted ceiling by Rubens was installed in 1635, however, it was felt that the smoke from the lamps might damage it, and the holding of

Entrance hall of the Queen's House.

Designed in 1622 by Inigo Jones, the Banqueting House in London was part of an immense scheme for a royal palace on the Thames at Whitehall. This painting by Canaletto, 1754, is in a private collection.

masques here was discontinued. The Banqueting House was the only part actually realized of an ambitious scheme by Jones for rebuilding the entire royal palace of Whitehall on the Thames. It was used for banquets offered by the King, for the reception of foreign embassies, and for all kinds of state and court ceremonies.

It was a hundred years before the Palladian movement took hold in England. Had Inigo Jones published his designs, there might have been a more general acceptance of his ideas at an earlier date. The intervening period saw the Civil War, the Fire of London, and, with the Restoration in 1660, the rise of Wren and the English baroque which gave such magnificent opportunities to Vanbrugh and Hawksmoor.

The south front of Wilton (1632) has often been attributed to Inigo Jones, and he may indeed have produced an outline plan for the third Earl of Pembroke. The drawing of the formal garden by Isaac de Caus shows that originally this front was to have been twice as long as it is, with a grandiose central portico. Part of the south front caught fire in 1647, and the reconstruction was entrusted to John Webb, Jones's nephew and assistant, who succeeded to his practice. The façade, which is terminated by the twin towers to be found on many Palladian buildings, has as

Wilton House, Salisbury. The south front (1632) is frequently attributed to Inigo Jones.

The double-cube room at the center of the south front of Wilton.

The house and formal garden, from the drawing by Isaac de Caus (1632), shows the south front of Wilton as twice its present length.

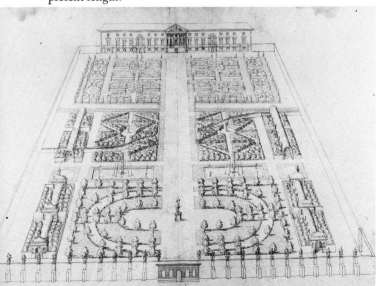

its centerpiece a Venetian window surmounted by recumbent figures and a heraldic shield. The grandiloquent double-cube room, dominated by the Van Dyck of the Herbert family, is in the center of this front.

Henry Herbert, ninth Earl of Pembroke, might well have shared the Earl of Burlington's sobriquet of the Architect Earl. He swept away the formal gardens, widened the Nadder River, and changed its course so that it flowed past the house at a greater distance. In 1737, with the help of Roger Morris, he built the Palladian Bridge. It was possibly inspired by the bridge published in the *Quattro Libri*, intended for the Rialto in Venice. The Wilton bridge is balanced, elegant, and of a calm serenity that was in marked contrast to the irascible temper of its inventor. It was copied three times in England: at Stowe, Prior Park, and Hagley, as well as at Tsarskoe Selo near St. Petersburg, and recently at Groussay outside Paris.

Pembroke was an accomplished architect. Thirteen years previously he had designed Marble Hill, Twickenham, for Henrietta Howard, Countess of Suffolk, with the help of Roger Morris, who put the plan into effect. She was supposedly the mistress of George II (he did refer to her in a letter as *"ma vieille maîtresse"*), and the King contributed £12,000 to the cost of the building. Mahogany was used in the interior here and at Houghton for the first time. In cruel surroundings and with a crinkled-tiled roof, Marble Hill has survived to this day and is open to the public:

The Palladian bridge designed by the ninth Earl of Pembroke in 1737 for Wilton.

Biddesden House, Andover, a Dutch–Palladian brick structure, was designed by an amateur architect in 1711.

it is one of the earliest villas in England. Lord Pembroke and Wilton create a link between the Palladianism of Jones and Webb and the true flowering of the movement in the early eighteenth century. In 1715 two books were published that were to have architectural repercussions throughout the country: Colen Campbell's *Vitruvius Britannicus* and Giacomo Leoni's edition of Palladio's *Quattro Libri*. At a stroke, the "artisan mannerist" style was shown up as clumsy, amateurish, and old-fashioned. No longer would the bricklayer and the master mason dictate the pattern that English architecture was to follow. A new professionalism was at hand, nurtured, strange to say, by a group of gifted amateurs of which Lord Pembroke was one.

The leader of this group was the Earl of Burlington and Cork, a Maecenas who devoted his life to the arts. When he traveled, he would hire one (or two) harpsichords at each stop, and his London house was an important center of artistic activity. His circle included Handel, Pope, Swift, and Berkeley. Leoni's version of Palladio was by no means a faithful reproduction, and many of his "corrections" completely altered the original drawings. Burlington did not approve, and caused an accurate version to be brought out by the architect Isaac Ware in 1738.

Alterations to Burlington House in London had been commissioned by Lord Burlington's mother, to be carried out by the architect James Gibbs while her son was on the Grand Tour. On the young Earl's return from the Continent, however, he found Campbell's *Vitruvius*, to which he had subscribed before his departure. This was the architect for him: Gibbs was dismissed and Campbell took his place. He put a new front on the seventeenth-century house, matched Gibbs's stables with other offices across the forecourt, and designed the entrance arch "agreeable to the Colonnade in the Court." Stutchbury, in his work on Campbell's architecture, suggests that this may mean that the colonnade was already standing when the arch was put up, but the statement could be taken otherwise.

Marble Hill, Twickenham, a Palladian villa on the Thames designed by Lord Pembroke (1724).

Whoever was responsible for its design, the forecourt of Burlington House must have been a wonderful sight. Horace Walpole described it thus:

> As we have few samples of architecture more antique and imposing than this colonnade, I cannot help mentioning the effect it had on myself. . . . Soon after my return from Italy I was invited to a ball at Burlington House. As I passed under the gate by night, it could not strike me. At daybreak, looking out of the window to see the sun rise, I was surprised with the vision of the colonnade that fronted me. It seemed one of those edifices in a fairy-tale that are raised by genii in a night's time.

Here was the inspiration of the forecourt of Leinster House, Dublin, and it is a sobering thought that both have been deliberately destroyed in the name of culture.

Mereworth Castle in Kent is a fairly close copy by Campbell of the Villa Rotonda, which the architect must have seen when he was at the University of Padua in 1697. Mereworth is a villa, built for entertaining at a reasonable distance from London, as opposed to a country estate that it might have taken two or three days to reach. This made it possible to give practically all the space to reception rooms, as bedroom accommodation was of secondary importance. It was built in 1722 for John Fane, afterward seventh Earl of Westmorland. He married Lady Mary Cavendish, granddaughter of the first Duke of Devonshire, in 1732. Campbell died in 1729, so that the pavilions that the Fanes found it necessary to add must be by another hand. Although not attached to the villa, they stand in such perfect relationship to it that it is tempting to imagine that Campbell might have made a rough draft of them before his death.

A balloon ascension in 1814 at Burlington House, from an engraving.

"The great Gate at Burlington House in Pickadilly." From Campbell's *Vitruvius Britannicus.*

Burlington House, London. This Palladification of an earlier house was completed by Colen Campbell, c. 1717. The painting, signed "Visentini et Zuccarelli/Fecerunt Venetis 1746," hangs in Windsor Castle. *Reproduced by gracious permission of Her Majesty the Queen.*

Mereworth Castle as shown in a painting by Visentini and Zuccarelli. *Reproduced by gracious permission of Her Majesty the Queen.*

Mereworth Castle was built in 1722 by Colen Campbell for Colonel the Hon. John Fane, M.P. Pavilions to either side were added in 1732, after Campbell's death.

The central rotunda of Mereworth, with plasterwork by Bagutti, was completed in 1725.

Houghton Hall, Norfolk, was built for Sir Robert Walpole, M.P., largely to Campbell's designs.

The elevation of Ebberston from Campbell's *Vitruvius Britannicus.*

Ebberston Lodge, Yorkshire, a miniature Palladian house by Campbell, built in 1718 for Sir William Thompson, M.P.

The south front and formal water gardens of Ebberston, from an early eighteenth-century
painting by an unknown hand.

Chiswick Villa, built by Lord Burlington in 1725 as an extension of Chiswick House for entertaining.

The garden front of Chiswick.

The gallery of Chiswick.

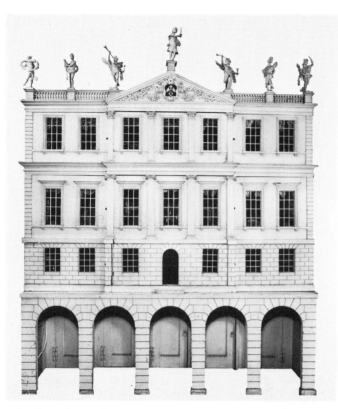

Sarah Lethiullier's doll's house, c. 1730. This little Palladian building was brought to Uppark, Sussex, by the bride of Sir Matthew Featherstonehaugh. Nine panels in the façade open into an equal number of rooms, each appropriately furnished. Archways in the stand below represent openings to the stables. The doll's house is a charming documentation in miniature of the taste of its time.

The Assembly Rooms, York, designed by Lord Burlington in 1730, based on the Egyptian Hall in the *Quattro Libri.*

Holkham Hall, Norfolk, built for the first Earl of Leicester in 1734 by William Kent.

In his introduction to *Vitruvius Britannicus* Campbell the Scot refers to the baroque as "extravagant, affected, and licentious." The interiors of his houses, however, are nothing if not ornate; it was the outside that was plain. The Palladians were the butt of much contemporary ridicule, and one of the charges leveled against them was that their houses were excessively dark due to the wide spaces between windows. Houghton in Norfolk is an instance of this. It was built by Campbell for Sir Robert Walpole in 1722. The east front is reminiscent of the long plain garden front at Wilton, although as built the end towers were given domes instead of pediments.

Ebberston Lodge, Yorkshire, now known as Ebberston Hall, was designed by Campbell in 1718 and is the smallest of all his houses. William Thompson, who commissioned it, lived only three miles away, and the little rusticated pavilion must have been built purely for entertaining, although "Lodge" seems to convey a sporting connotation. In 1905 the cupola was removed, and the loggia was later filled in to form the dining room; the water gardens have long since disappeared. Ebberston is a masterpiece on a miniature scale, and Campbell has managed to give it qualities of nobility and grandeur often lacking in far larger houses.

The Architect Earl tired of Colen Campbell, from whom he had learned so much, and who had given his London house the first Palladian façade in the city. Burlington was soon engaged in several architectural enterprises of his own invention, with Henry Flitcroft as his draftsman. Burlington befriended William Kent, who lived at Burlington House for no less than thirty years, until his death in 1748. Kent was at the time a painter of historical scenes and did not take up

51

architecture until after 1730. Burlington possessed a large old house and land at Chiswick, near London, and in 1725 designed a villa as an extension of the house. He used the villa only to entertain his friends amid sumptuous surroundings, but always intended to keep the old house for living quarters, and designed a passage linking the two buildings. Palladian houses were "more for looking at than living in." The villa at Chiswick is a smaller version of the Rotonda, but with very important differences. The central core is octagonal, not circular; there is only one portico, and the garden elevation with its three Palladian windows is strikingly original. The stark, almost neoclassical lines recall Scamozzi's Rocca Pisana rather than the Rotonda. The exterior is correct but somewhat cold, in contrast to the human scale and rich variety of decoration to be found within.

In 1730 Burlington built the Assembly Rooms in York, where he was a powerful landowner and had been Lord Lieutenant for fifteen years. It was a meeting place used for receptions and balls during the "season." It is sometimes forgotten that provincial towns far smaller than York enjoyed a season: London was out of reach for all but a few. Burlington took the plan from the *Quattro Libri*, which illustrates a so-called Egyptian Hall; in fact the design owes little to Egypt except its name. No other town in England can boast anything to equal these assembly rooms. Francis Drake, in the 1788 edition of *Eboracum*, writes:

> The grand room is an antique Egyptian hall, from Palladio, 112 feet in length, the breadth 40, and 40 the height. This room consists of two orders, viz. the lower part, with 44 columns and capitals, and a famous cornice, complete the Corinthian order. The upper part is after the Composite, richly beautiful with festoons, imitating oak leaves and acorns, likewise a beautiful cornice, curiously enriched with carved work. There are 44 windows. From the top of this room depend 13 lustres of blown glass, each carrying 18 candles; but more particularly in the centre is a lustre, most curiously carved, being the gift of the right hon. the earl of Burlington. The entrance is at the east end.

William Kent was a competent decorative painter, a superb designer of furniture, and a revolutionary landscape gardener. He "leapt the fence, and saw that all nature was a garden"; his natural landscapes at Rousham and Stowe, although studded with temples, statuary, and eye-catchers, were among the first instances of "round the corner" gardening so different from the formal French or Dutch layouts. Kent turned to architecture in his mid-forties.

Holkham, in Norfolk, was designed by Kent for Thomas Coke, first Earl of Leicester, in 1734. It is built of a narrow yellow brick in imitation of that used in ancient Rome, and time has given its immense façade and four attendant wings a greenish hue. Like Houghton, the interior is incredibly grand, and both houses contain magnificent pictures and furniture. Both have been notably improved in recent years, for at Holkham the plate-glass windows with their dull Victorian stare have windowpanes once more, and at Houghton the staircase on the east front has been replaced to Colen Campbell's original design. These are the prodigy houses of the Palladian era.

Like Holkham, Badminton, in Gloucestershire, is the great house of a large estate and merits a book of its own, but unlike its fellows, Badminton reached its final grandeur of proportion and detail by a process of evolution over a considerable period of time. There is evidence that the great hall was inserted between the wings of a sixteenth-century house by the first Duke of Beaufort, during the reign of Charles II. The north doorway, the corner cupolas, and the curious pediment were added for the third Duke after 1740, almost certainly to the designs of William Kent, in order to give emphasis to the central block. Kent also designed Worcester Lodge, which stands at the formal entrance to the park. The upper story of the lodge contains the "room where the Duke dines in summer," and from which he could look up the avenue to the great north front of Badminton House, three miles distant.

The Palladian houses of England have one thing in common—they are completely new-built, and in the rare instance that an earlier structure forms part of a building it is kept well out of sight. Such purity was uncommon in England, where the charm of the country house often

Badminton House, Gloucestershire, the north front, from the painting by Canaletto, c. 1748.

consists in the collective additions made over the years according to the fashion of the day. The style was associated for a time with the new rich; the great banking houses of Hoare and Child were among the first to favor it. Lords Burlington and Pembroke, however, who made Palladianism fashionable, derived their wealth from land. It would naturally appeal to a person building from scratch to choose the most up-to-date style, whereas an established family might hesitate to pull down a house furnished with the laughter of the years.

"Your Lordship knows this barren bleak island too well to expect any news from it with your notice. The most remarkable thing now going on is a house of Mr. Conolly's at Castletown. . . . I hope it will be an ornament to the country."

—George Berkeley to John Percival, Earl of Egmont, July 1722

IRELAND

In Ireland the country house has always enjoyed more purity of style. Little or no domestic architecture survives from the Elizabethan or Jacobean periods, and the Famine in the 1840s put a stop to Victorian "improvement." A love of show inherent in the Irish nature often led to overbuilding; size of house was an indication of family importance, and as a type the villa was too constricting to achieve popularity. On occasion the funds ran dry before the house was completed, and in the case of Castlecoole, Co. Fermanagh, designed by James Wyatt in 1790, it was left to the following generation to complete the furnishing. As a result, heavy Regency furniture out of character with the delicate interior was specially made for the house. If the wherewithal to complete and furnish the Irish country house was lacking, it follows that alterations and additions were a luxury seldom embarked upon.

The Palladian invasion of Ireland began with the building of Castletown, Co. Kildare, in 1722. The Rt. Hon. William Conolly, Member of Parliament for Ballyshannon, as Speaker of the Irish House of Commons needed a residence near Dublin and built his great house on land acquired beside the River Liffey twelve miles from the city. It remains very much as he built it, the gray-white façade of "stupendous monotony," the curved colonnades leading to wings of a golden stone. The architect had long been forgotten, as is so often the case in Ireland, but it has now been established beyond reasonable doubt that Alessandro Galilei was responsible, best known for the façade he added to St. John in Lateran, Rome.

Castletown had a remarkable influence on the shape and layout of the Irish country house for years to come, although in terms of size and grandeur it has never been rivaled. Galilei left Ireland, doubting there was an opportunity for an architect to prosper in Berkeley's "barren, bleak island," and some of the building of Castletown and the ordering of its interior were carried out by the brilliant young Irish architect Edward Lovett Pearce. Born in 1699, Pearce was knighted for his

The entrance hall of Castletown, with detailing by Sir Edward Lovett Pearce, an Irish architect who had been to Italy and was imbued with Palladian ideas.

OVERLEAF: Castletown (1722), Co. Kildare: designed by Alessandro Galilei for the Rt. Hon. William Conolly, Speaker of the Irish House of Commons.

Niche in the front hall of Bellamont.

The drawing room ceiling of Bellamont has seventeenth-century overtones.

work on the Parliament House in Dublin, the noblest public building in the city to this day, for which Speaker Conolly laid the foundation stone in 1728. Pearce was appointed Surveyor General in 1730, but lived for only three more years.

Bellamont Forest (c. 1730) was built for the Cootes, Earls of Bellamont, in a part of County Cavan of great natural beauty. Pearce was their cousin and a natural choice as architect. The arrangement of the façade, the treatment of the upper story, and its lighting through a cupola overhead derive from the Rotonda. The basic proportions of the building, the floor plan, and the Doric portico are taken from the Villa Pisani at Montagnana, which is a smaller counterpart of the Villa Cornaro. Pearce originally suggested a recessed portico, but it was decided to eliminate this as a waste of space and unsuited to the climate. Moreover, it would have rendered the house less defensible in case of attack. Castle strongholds had not survived as dwellings into the seventeenth century for nothing, and carved stone gunports are to be found covering the front door of many an otherwise innocent-looking country house. Bellamont has a richly decorated interior with elaborate plasterwork, some of it seventeenth century in character. In the hall, marble busts of the Cootes, disguised as Roman emperors, gaze at each other from their niches across the black-and-white-squared stone floor. It is the best example in Ireland of a Palladian villa.

Bellamont Forest, Co. Cavan, designed by Pearce in 1730 for his cousin Thomas Coote, is the foremost example in Ireland of a Palladian villa.

CARTON. *The Seat of the Rig.* Hon.*ble the Earl of* KILDARE

Carton, Co. Kildare. An engraving of 1752, before the curved colonnades were removed. Designed by Richard Castle in 1739, the façade was modeled on Castletown, only four miles distant.

A German architect, Richard Castle, was the effective heir to Pearce's practice. He was a native of Hesse-Kassel, and little is known of his life or work before his arrival in Ireland in 1728, when he was befriended by Pearce, who gave him the following warm recommendation: "I know nobody in this Town whom I could employ capable of drawing from designs of this nature but one Person, and he, indeed, has done them infinite justice, his name is Castle, he is at present employed in building a House for Sir Gustavus Hume near Enniskillen but I hope will find more and constant employment."

Castle must have been acquainted with Lord Burlington and his circle. His correct "English" Palladianism can have had no other origins—certainly not in his native land. He established the Palladian style in Ireland, and his massive winged houses seem as much at home there as they would in the dusty, flat plain of the Veneto. He has been accused of being a rather heavy-handed architect, but it could have been reassuring to those building so soon after the Battle of the Boyne to favor more massive proportions than would be found in England at that date. It may have given them a feeling of security, an illusion that their society was destined to endure.

Carton, Co. Kildare, only four miles from Castletown, was built to the designs of Richard Castle in 1739. It is easy to see how much he owed to the earlier house by a comparison of the

The great baroque ceiling of the saloon of Carton was executed by the Francini brothers for the nineteenth Earl of Kildare, whose son was made Duke of Leinster in 1766.

The north elevation of Leinster House in a recent photograph.

façades. Like Castletown, Carton is near Dublin, and the house and park were seen and admired by a constant stream of visitors. One of these, Lady Caroline Dawson, who stayed here in 1778, writes:

> Everything seems to go on in great state here, the Duchess appears in a sack and hoop and diamonds in an afternoon; French horns playing at every meal; and such quantities of plate, etc., that one would imagine oneself in a palace. And there are servants without end. That morning they drove us all over the park, which is really very fine; though all done by his father—therefore no wood of any growth. But there is a fine river with rocks, etc. . . . It is not the fashion at Carton to play cards. The ladies sit and work, and the gentlemen lollop about and go to sleep—at least the Duke does, for he snored so loud the other night that we all got into a great fit of laughing and waked him.

Carton was built for the nineteenth Earl of Kildare, whose son became the first Duke of Leinster in 1766, and it was for him that Castle built the great town house now known as Leinster House. The great colonnaded forecourt he gave to Leinster House in 1745 bore more than a passing resemblance to that at Burlington House, particularly in his original plan. The architect must have remained on a good footing with his patron, for when he died in 1751 he was staying at Carton and was in the course of writing a letter to the carpenter at the Dublin house. His public commissions in

North elevation of Leinster House.

Leinster House, Dublin, built in 1745 by Richard Castle, was originally known as Kildare House. The illustration is from Roque's map of Dublin.

G. Smith Delin.

KILDARE HOUSE

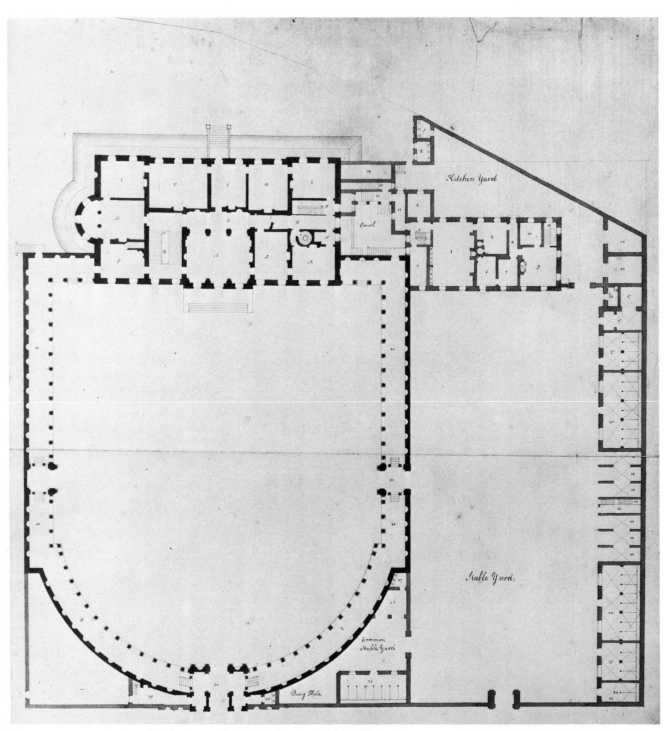

The noble forecourt of Castle's plan for Leinster House was swept away in the last century when the National Library and National Museum were built.

The Villa Malcontenta.

The Villa Rotonda.

The Villa Maser.

Mereworth Castle.

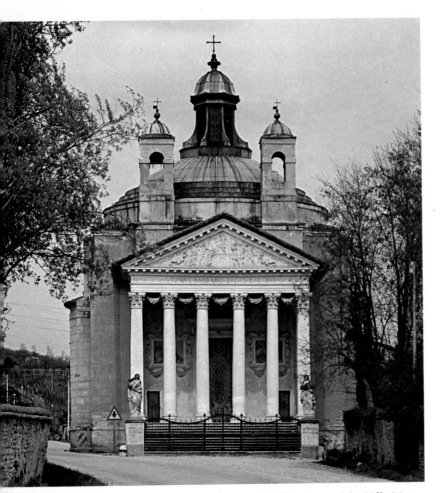

The *Tempietto* of the Villa Maser.

Kilshannig.

The nymphaeum of the Villa Maser.

Castletown.

The Great Hall of Castletown.

Mountain granite from the nearby Golden Hill Quarry was used to build Russborough in 1745.

The entrance gates of Russborough, Co. Wicklow, are typical of Castle's correct Palladian proportions.

The decoration on the staircase walls has been described as "the ravings of a maniac"; the artist's identity is unknown.

Russborough's seven-hundred-foot façade.

the capital include the Printing House, a little Doric temple, and the Dining Hall at Trinity College. Tyrone House and Clanwilliam House in Dublin were designed by him, and Powerscourt and Westport in the country, together with bridges, churches, and the domed Market House in Dunlavin, Co. Wicklow. With Teutonic energy that must have startled the Irish, his practice extended from coast to coast. He was a great perfectionist—if he didn't like the way a building was going on, he would insist that it be taken down to the ground and begun anew.

Of his houses, Russborough, Co. Wicklow, comes closest to perfection. The façade is seven hundred feet in length, curved colonnades lead to wings in the now familiar pattern, and there are yards to either side in perfect symmetry. The agricultural complex is just as appropriate to Co. Wicklow as it is to the Villa Badoer from which this layout is derived. It suited the pretensions of those building at this time to make their façades as long as possible, pressing into service outbuildings that would otherwise be yards separate from the house. Russborough (1745) is one of the last houses Castle designed, and its façade has none of the heaviness of which he has been accused. The interior, however, is encrusted with florid plaster decoration. Nothing is known of the artists in plaster who were let loose on the reception rooms; the quality is variable, but for imagination and sheer exuberance the staircase decoration is without equal.

Palladianism and the rococo stayed alive in provincial Ireland long after the dead hand of Adam had reached the capital. An Italian architect, Davis Ducart, was one of those responsible, and he lived on well into the nineteenth century without bothering to come to terms with contemporary fashion. Kilshannig, Co. Cork, was built by him in 1765 for Abraham Devonsher, a Cork banker, and it has plaster by Paul and Philip Francini so that it is Italian in more than its architecture. Devonsher must have been a sporting banker, for he insisted on a lugubrious-looking plaster fox being placed below the dead game in the coving of the dining room. The Francinis' figured plasterwork is to be found at Carton, at Castletown, and at Russborough, where the saloon ceiling can be attributed to them on stylistic grounds.

The Genealogical Office, formerly the Office of Arms, is the centerpiece of the north side of the upper yard in Dublin Castle. A small Heraldic Museum has been installed in the room from which the crown jewels were stolen at the time of Edward VII's visit in 1907. The work of tracing family pedigrees goes on here. The exact date of the building is not known; it is not shown on Brooking's map of 1728 but does appear in an engraving by Tudor of 1752. The top floor is a nineteenth-century addition, accomplished without putting the composition off balance. In the old days a military band used to play in the loggia when there was a parade in the courtyard below.

◄ The richness of the interior of Russborough is without equal in Ireland.

The saloon ceiling. The Francini brothers' plasterwork in Kilshannig is their finest in Ireland.

Plasterwork on the Kilshannig dining room ceiling.

Details of the Kilshannig saloon ceiling.

OVERLEAF: Kilshannig, Co. Cork, was designed in 1765 by the Italian Davis Ducart for Abraham Devonsher, a Cork banker and country gentleman.

Genealogical Office, Dublin Castle. Architect and date unknown.

The arches on either side carry lead statues of Justice and Mars by Van Nost; Justice's scales used to tilt when it rained, eliciting sardonic comments from the Dublin populace on the subject of British justice. The authorities apparently got wind of this and ordered holes to be drilled in the pans so that the rain could run out.

Lucan House, Co. Dublin (1775), stands beside the Liffey, which, in terms of the buildings along her banks, is the Irish equivalent of the Brenta. It was designed in the Palladian manner by an amateur architect, Agmondisham Vesey, who was named Professor of Architecture in Dr. Johnson's Utopian university. He lived there with his wife, a celebrated blue-stocking, who declared she felt "like a parrot in a cage" in her round sitting room. The interior has the Adamesque roundels and swags that are to be expected at that date. Elegant but restrained, the new style sounded the death knell of the magnificent plaster flourishes of the 1750s. Lucan House, a pure Palladian villa, makes a suitable residence for the Italian Ambassador to Ireland.

Lucan House, Co. Dublin, designed in 1775 by Agmondisham Vesey, an amateur architect.
A pure Palladian villa, it is now the Italian Embassy.

The house of General Wade in London, built in 1723 by Lord Burlington, as shown in the painting by Visentini and Zuccarelli. *Reproduced by gracious permission of Her Majesty the Queen.*

An elevation drawn by Palladio. Purchased by Lord Burlington, the drawing forms the basis of his design for General Wade's house in Piccadilly.

The Provost's House, Trinity College, Dublin, 1759. John Smyth borrowed the elevation from Campbell's *Vitruvius Britannicus* and added wings of his own invention. Smyth was at the same time building St. Thomas's Church in Dublin, since destroyed, which was an adaptation of the Redentore, with curved sweeps.

Derby House, Salem, Massachusetts, in an unexecuted design by Charles Bulfinch, 1795. Samuel McIntire was later commissioned to build the house, which has been demolished.

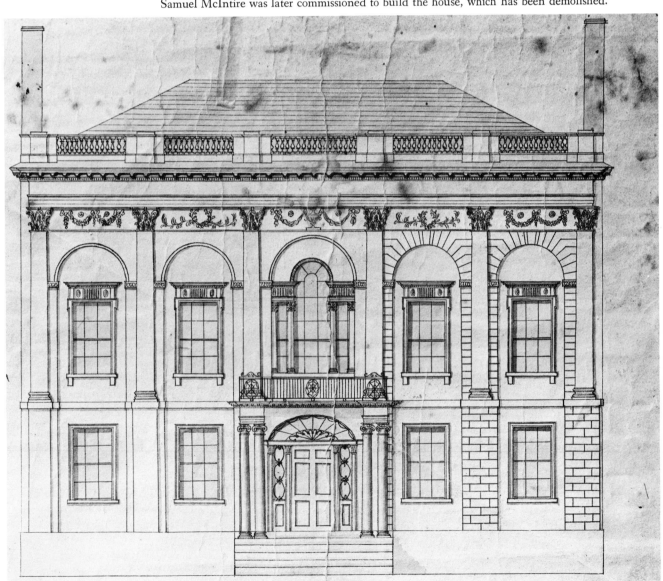

NORTH AMERICA

George Berkeley, the author and philosopher, landed at Newport, Rhode Island, in January 1729. He was a Senior Fellow of Trinity College, Dublin, Dean of Derry, and would later become Bishop of Cloyne. A friend of Lord Burlington, he boasted, "you must know I pretend to an uncommon skill in architecture." Berkeley had been to Italy, and wrote of the Pantheon, "The eye is never weary with viewing," but of St. Peter's, "The Church itself I find a thousand faults with." He went on to say, "there is not any one modern building in Rome that pleases me, except the wings of the Capitol built by Michael Angelo and the colonnade of Bernini's before St. Peter's." Significantly, he admired "the little round [church] in the place where St. Peter was beheaded built by Bramante, which is very pretty and built like an ancient temple." This is the only building neither designed by Palladio nor taken from classical antiquity to be included in the *Quattro Libri*.

In 1722, when he was at Trinity College, Berkeley was consulted by Speaker Conolly, who was just then starting to build Castletown; Berkeley did not offer a design, however, "because several have been made by several hands," and "I do not approve of a work conceived by many heads." In 1725 he published *A Proposal for the better supplying of Churches on our foreign plantations, and for converting the Savage Americans to Christianity, by a College to be erected on the Summer Islands, otherwise called the Isles of Bermuda.* Berkeley's *Proposal* provided for a town to be built near the new college in a manner resembling the garden suburbs of today. The college itself was to be on a circular plan. An "academical circus" of fellows' houses was to be in the center; a residential circus was planned outside this, with shops and artificers' houses on the outer ring. This visionary design anticipated Ledoux's Ville de Chaux and Jefferson's University of Virginia by many years. Berkeley was promised £20,000 for the undertaking; he set sail with his bride for Rhode Island in 1728.

Soon after their arrival, Berkeley purchased an old farmhouse three miles from Newport, which he christened Whitehall. It stood in a valley, under a hill commanding a broad prospect, and

Doorcase. Plate 56 from *The Designs of Inigo Jones*, Volume I, 1727.

Whitehall, Rhode Island. The modest doorcase on Bishop Berkeley's house
heralds the arrival of the Palladian style in New England.

he declined to build on the eminence lest the view become commonplace through continual famil-
iarity. His chair and writing equipment stood in a natural grotto overlooking the beach. It was here
that he wrote the famous lines:

> Westward the star of Empire takes its way;
> The four first acts already past,
> A fifth shall close the drama with the day:
> Time's noblest offering is the last.

Alciphron, published in 1732, was also written at Whitehall, and contains a tribute to the Earl of
Burlington: "Crito . . . observed that he knew an English nobleman who in the prime of his life
professed a liberal art, and is the first man of his profession in the world; and that he was very sure
that he had more pleasure from the excercise of that elegant art than from any sensual enjoyment
within the power of one of the largest fortunes and most bountiful spirits in Great Britain." Later
in the dialogue is the following paraphrase from Palladio himself: "Euphranor: And, to make the
proportions just, must not those mutual relations of size and shape in the parts be such as shall make
the whole complete and perfect of its kind?"

The promised funds for his college were not forthcoming, and Berkeley returned to England
in 1731. He must have remembered his sojourn in the New World with affection, however, for he
sent an organ to Trinity Church, Newport, where he had often preached, and a thousand volumes
of his library to Yale University. He also presented the deeds of his Rhode Island property to Yale,
the income from which was directed to the support of "three deserving students."

CAPITOLE de ROME

Capitoline Hill, Rome, as replanned by Michelangelo in 1546. Woodcut from *La Géométrie Pratique*, Plate XLIII.

Whitehall is the only house for which Berkeley can have been responsible. The entrance appears to have been taken from the Ionic doorcase shown in Plate 56, Volume I, of *The Designs of Inigo Jones*, published by William Kent in 1727, just before Berkeley came to America. This work would have been familiar to him at Trinity; he may even have owned a copy. He was particularly interested in doors, discoursing on their proportions in *Alciphron*. In order to achieve the correct proportions for the front door at Whitehall, he had to make the left panel blind, with a solid wall behind it. This modest doorcase may be the first expression of the Palladian idiom to find its way to New England. It is chaste by comparison with the baroque doorways of Trinity Church and the Colony House in Newport with their naïve scroll pediments.

By 1743 Whitehall had become an inn and a popular halting place for summer visitors. It was the first colonial house to be illustrated photographically in a national magazine, appearing in the *New York Sketch Book* in 1874, where the emphasis was placed on the picturesque qualities of the shingled roof. In 1899 the Colonial Dames of America obtained a 999-year lease on the then ruinous building and began a program of preservation and restoration.

St. James' Church, Goose Creek, is the earliest Anglican congregation in South Carolina outside of Charleston. It was founded by settlers who, like the Draytons of Drayton Hall, came from Barbados, and resembles the churches being built in the West Indies at the time, with one somewhat remarkable difference. The main entrance is framed by a simple Doric doorcase, surmounted by an awkward pediment now embellished by a thrice-restored "Pelican in her Piety." This unusual detail is the emblem of the Society for the Propagation of the Gospel. The doorcase at St.

St. James' Church (1711), Goose Creek, South Carolina, in a photograph made before 1895. The pelican symbol is absent, and the frieze was later altered.

James' Church heralds the arrival of classicism in the Low Country, as does the doorway at Whitehall, Rhode Island, in New England. The pattern books that were available no doubt made their way to Charles Towne via Barbados.

Drayton Hall, on the Ashley River above Charleston, South Carolina, remained in the Drayton family from the time it was built in 1738 until 1974, when it passed into the hands of the National Trust for Historic Preservation. This house has been described by Samuel Chamberlain as "very probably the finest untouched example of Georgian architecture still standing in America." The only complete plantation house still remaining on the Ashley, it has miraculously escaped the devastations of earthquake, fire, and war that have overtaken its fellows. It was spared the holocaust of Sherman's march to the sea because Dr. Drayton converted it into a pesthouse for Negroes stricken with smallpox. Even in peacetime, fire has always been the deadliest threat to isolated country places; the fact that neither electricity, heat, nor plumbing has been introduced into Drayton Hall has spared it the dangers of overtaxed flues, faulty wiring, and careless maintenance that have taken their toll elsewhere.

The Draytons came to the Carolinas from Barbados in 1679 and settled upriver from Charles Towne Landing. In 1680 the original encampment at the Landing was transplanted to a new site on the Cooper River, where a walled city was under construction. Before the turn of the century, and for some years thereafter, protection from Indian and Spanish attackers was a necessity on the Ashley. By 1738, however, the Hon. John Drayton, member of His Majesty's Council, felt

Bremo. Painting by Edward Troye.

Clarendon Court. Painting by Felix Kelly (detail). The artist has transposed the house to face the ocean. ▶

The Pavilion. Painting by Felix Kelly (detail).

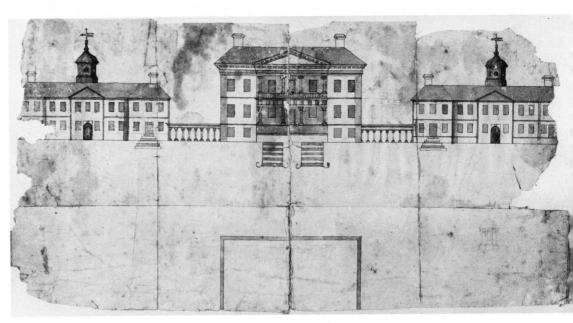

Drayton Hall, South Carolina, in an architectural drawing found in the house.

An early photograph of Drayton Hall. The flankers have since been taken down.

sufficiently secure to begin to build on river property he had lately acquired. Drayton and his architect, whose name is not known, must have had access to the pattern books available in the Colonies; perhaps those in the collection of Joseph Wragg, a fellow member of the Council, who possessed an architectural library remarkable for the time.

The double portico *in antis* facing the land recalls Palladio's Villa Cornaro. It leads into the great hall, where the overmantel is taken from a plate in William Kent's *Designs of Inigo Jones*, published in 1727, which reproduces "A Chimney-piece at the Right Honourable Sir *Robert Walpole's* at Houghton" that adorns the great Stone Hall. Drayton Hall is built of brick laid in

The house built in 1738 to the designs of an unidentified architect.

"A Chimney-Piece at the Right Honourable Sir Robert Walpole's at Houghton . . ." Plate 64 from *The Designs of Inigo Jones*.

The paneled staircase of Drayton Hall being measured by the Historic American Buildings Survey, 1974.

Flemish bond; the Doric and Ionic columns of the portico are of Portland stone and were imported ready-carved from England. Architecturally in advance of its time, Drayton Hall was begun three years before Malbone Hall near Newport, which, although considered to be the finest residence in the Colonies, was, according to Alexander Hamilton, "not extraordinary for the architecture, being a clumsy Dutch modell."

The riverside entrance opens into the paneled stair hall beyond which lie the great hall and the west portico. The spectacular double staircase leads to the large drawing room and the bedrooms on the upper floor. The small drawing room, dining room, chamber, and library are on the main floor, and the service rooms are at ground level. Elaborate mantelpieces, paneling, cornices, and plasterwork appear throughout the house, and furniture that has remained in the family demonstrates the elegance of eighteenth-century life at Drayton Hall. At the beginning of the nineteenth century two of the original mantels were taken out and Adam replacements substituted. When the family papers have been thoroughly explored, more information about the interior will surely come to light, and it is particularly desirable that this should emerge now, when restoration of this superb house is in sight.

The building must have been largely complete in 1742 when William Henry Drayton, the Revolutionary Chief Justice of South Carolina, was born there. It continued to serve the family as a residence until the removal of the lead roof, which was cast into bullets during the War Between the States, causing some upstairs ceilings to fall through weather damage. Fortunately, little other harm was done. The discovery of phosphates on family property provided funds for replacing the

The entrance hall of Drayton Hall.

Detail of overmantel at Drayton Hall.

roof and for some exterior work and landscaping. Drayton Hall, the oldest surviving Palladian house in the country, belonged to seven generations of Draytons. Under the auspices of the National Trust, it will be maintained and restored as an important part of the American heritage.

Berkeley, during his residence at Newport, is said to have suggested the formation of a literary society. Not long after his departure one was formed, and became in time the Redwood Library Company, named for Abraham Redwood, who in 1747 gave £500 for the purchase of books. The town of Newport subscribed £5000 for a building, and the following year one Henry Collins provided a suitable site. A memorandum, dated February 6, 1749, states: "in consideration of the Builders conforming to the sd. Draught drawn by Mr. Peter Harrison, and following his directions as to all the Alterations herein mentioned," which is evidence that Harrison was the author of the design.

Peter Harrison, with his brother Joseph, emigrated to Newport in 1739. Born in York in 1716, he was fourteen when Burlington's Assembly Rooms were going up. Architecture was ever an interest of his, along with woodcarving, surveying, and seamanship. In Rhode Island the Harrisons went to work for a merchant trader whose ships carried goods to and from England. Joseph Harrison was already a captain, Peter about to receive his ticket, and their rise in position carried with it opportunities to sail to South Carolina as well as to England. On his first journey to Charles Towne in 1742, Peter may have seen Drayton Hall, just then completed. He was entertained, then, and again in 1747, by Gabriel Manigault, grandfather of the architect of that name.

Engraving from a nineteenth-century bookplate of the Redwood Library, Newport, Rhode Island, designed in 1749 by Peter Harrison.

Like his friend Joseph Wragg, Manigault had a comprehensive library which must have included architectural volumes. Leaving Charles Towne after this visit, Harrison made a last trip to England, where he spent his time traveling and collecting books and furniture.

On his return to Newport he became engaged in the Redwood Library project. He had by that time acquired the nucleus of an architectural library which, when he died in 1775, was one of the finest in the country. These volumes provided him with ideas for the new library and other architectural essays to follow. The Redwood Library as conceived by Harrison owes nothing to contemporary American building styles, but springs from English example, following the principles of Palladio. It echoes the elevation of S. Giorgio, which had been used by Burlington and Kent for garden buildings. It is the first temple-form building in America. The entrance façade follows closely the headpiece of Book IV of Edward Hoppus's *Andrea Palladio* (1735–1736), while the rear elevation is adapted from the garden front at Chiswick, although Harrison had originally drawn it with only one Venetian window. The Library is a frame building, the exterior "covered with Pine Plank worked in Imitation of Rustick." The great hall within, reminiscent of the Egyptian Hall in York, provides space for bookshelves and for reading. The building has been enlarged three times and still serves its original purpose admirably.

The Redwood Library is a monument to Peter Harrison, America's first known architect. He afterward designed King's Chapel in Boston, a summerhouse for the Redwood estate, Touro Synagogue, and the Brick Market in Newport, each of which reflects a dependence upon Palladian sources. Carl Bridenbaugh suggests that he may also have designed St. Michael's, Charles Towne,

Redwood Library. Behind the main building may be seen the later additions.

The entrance hall of the library.

The second Capitol at Williamsburg.

Tazewell Hall, Virginia. By the time this photograph was taken in the 1940s the house had been mutilated.

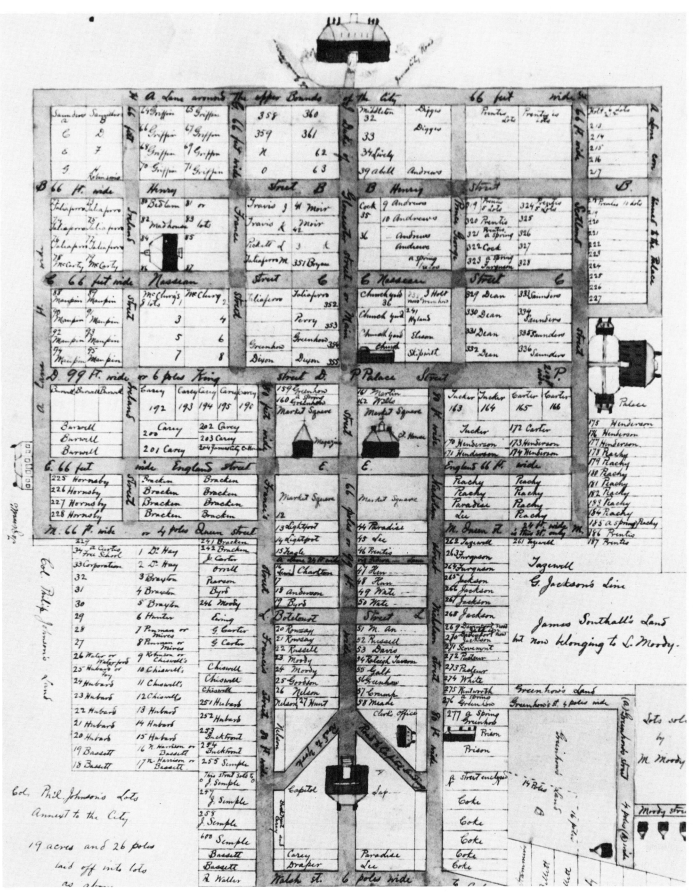

The building, before 1737, of Tazewell Hall in Williamsburg closed one of the main axes of the town.

The entrance front of Tazewell Hall is a subtle Palladian composition.

The entrance hall, two stories high, of Tazewell.

The paneled drawing room.

The south front of the restored Tazewell Hall overlooks the James River.

Gunston Hall, Lorton, Virginia, built before 1775 by George Mason.

which was not started until 1752, five years after his last visit to the city. Although Harrison did not return to the South, a number of influential South Carolinians were accustomed to sail up to New England in summer. They may have seen and admired the Redwood Library and King's Chapel, and renewed their acquaintance with the architect.

On April 20, 1760, he became the Collector for the Port of Newhaven, a post he held until his death in April 1775. This was a period of extreme tension between the Tories and the radical New Haven Whigs. The *Connecticut Journal* ends its obituary tribute: "in his death learning appears veil'd: and the fine art of architecture has now in America no standard." Nevertheless, six months after he died, the Customs House and his home were plundered by a "Riotous Mob." His widow submitted a claim for losses, including "a large and elegant Library of Books containing to the best of my remembrance between Six and Seven Hundred Volumes, besides manuscripts and a large Collection of Drawings, all of which were destroyed." Peter Harrison's buildings are all that remain of his genius.

The second Capitol at Williamsburg was built in 1752 to replace the original, built in 1700 and destroyed by fire in 1747. After the state capital removed to Richmond, the second Capitol became a school and in 1852 it likewise was burned. Colonial Williamsburg elected to restore the earlier building. The second Capitol is shown here with its naïve Palladian frontispiece; Thomas Jefferson commented upon it in his *Notes on the State of Virginia*:

> The capitol is a light and airy structure, with a portico in front of two orders, the lower of which, being Doric, is tolerably just in its proportions and ornaments, save only that the intercolonations are too large. The upper is Ionic, much too small for that on which it is mounted, its ornaments not proper to the order, nor proportioned within themselves. It is crowned with a pediment, which is too high for its span. Yet, on the whole, it is the most pleasing piece of architecture we have.

Sir John Randolph, the only native Virginian ever to have been knighted, was Clerk of the House of Burgesses at Williamsburg. He died in 1737, but his Williamsburg residence has remained *in situ* facing the Court House Green. The central part, which provides the main entrance, was built by Sir John to join two separate houses. The interior contains the finest paneled rooms in the town, which, together with the marble mantels and great stairway, set it apart from its more modest neighbors. It provided an appropriate setting for Sir John's large library, comparable to that of William Byrd of Westover, and for his collection of historical manuscripts.

The Palladian movement in England was essentially Whiggish, and Sir John was loyal to the Crown. His principles were inherited by his young son John, who built Tazewell Hall after his marriage in 1751, but returned to England in 1755 rather than remain in a rebellious Virginia.

The vistas that close on the major buildings at Williamsburg impart an air of dignity and order to the town. One of them ends at the Wren Building of The College of William and Mary, another at the Capitol, and a cross-axis terminates at the Governor's Palace. Tazewell Hall was built to close a fourth vista at the end of South England Street. It is no longer there.

There were pattern books available to help John Randolph in his designs. Thomas Waterman in *The Mansions of Virginia* has suggested that there are several interior features influenced by

The Palladian Room of Gunston Hall is embellished with woodcarving by William Buckland.

Palladio Londinensis, 1734. He states: "Both flanking rooms are fully panelled with chimney breast projecting from the end walls. . . . The entablatures traverse the length of the breast where the architrave and cushion frieze are dropped. This cushion frieze occurs in almost all the houses showing the influence of *Palladio Londinensis*, but here is broader and less convex than most examples."

The chief glory of the house is the Great Hall, which occupies the entire central block. It may have been inspired by Burlington's York Assembly Rooms, borrowed from the Egyptian Hall of Vitruvius as interpreted by Palladio. The fenestration follows the Burlington engravings (*Eboracum*, 1736 edition) with clerestory windows to front and rear, but is without windows at either side due to the hipped roofs over the wings. Later, pilasters were installed, which tradition says were taken from the first theatre in America when it was removed from beside the Palace Green in 1769. Randolph had studied law in London, loved his books and his music (he played the violin at the Palace in Williamsburg together with his cousin Thomas Jefferson and the Governor), and was devoted to his garden. He was the author of *A Treatise on Gardening by a Virginia Gentleman*. When he left Williamsburg for the last time, a deed of trust was drawn up, clearly identifying the house and including an inventory and other relevant descriptive documents.

The house was acquired by John Tazewell in 1778 and has since carried his name. In 1836 one wing was removed, and at the same time a floor was inserted in the Great Hall and the sides raised a story. The central portion was moved in 1908 to face the street, newly extended to provide access to a development on the plantation beyond. Colonial Williamsburg took title to the building in 1927, but did not undertake its restoration. In 1954 it was purchased from the foundation by Delegate and Mrs. Lewis A. McMurran, Jr.; the building was dismantled and the eighteenth-century parts stored while research proceeded. Reconstruction on the present site overlooking the James River commenced in 1964. The original flooring, paneling, and hardware, together with the fragments from the theatre, have been restored to their proper places. The Great Hall once more rises to its full height, and marble mantels have been installed to replace the lost originals. Tazewell Hall today shows respect for the memory of John Randolph and the elegance of his taste.

Gunston Hall, Lorton, Virginia, has a Queen Anne exterior, with a steeply pitched roof, tall chimneys, and dormer windows. The interior, however, is of considerable refinement, and gives the impression of being later than the house. It was the property of George Mason, who, despising local talent, brought over from England in 1755 a joiner–carpenter to finish the interior. This craftsman was William Buckland, who had just completed his apprenticeship in London. Buckland gave Gunston Hall an up-to-date interior, and the admiration accorded his elaborate carved woodwork must have been the foundation of his successful career. There is little doubt that, given a free hand, Buckland would have built a Palladian house here, but the bones of Gunston Hall already existed, and as an indentured novice, aged twenty-one, he was hardly in a position to criticize his new master's creation, let alone suggest that he replace it with something more in the latest fashion. So Buckland had to content himself with a Palladian porch, and insisted on plain, not paneled, wall surfaces—a modest enough indication of his architectural talents. George Mason did well by his country in bringing this young man across the Atlantic. Buckland married and settled down in Virginia, establishing a successful practice there and in Maryland.

Gunston Hall has a geometric boxwood garden, restored by the Garden Club of Virginia, that stretches out toward the edge of the grounds whence there is a sharp descent to the Potomac. The river was the main thoroughfare for these plantations, and the garden front of Gunston Hall faces upstream in the direction of Mount Vernon, five miles to the northeast.

Carlyle House, Alexandria, Virginia, was the scene of an important meeting on April 14, 1755, attended by five Royal Governors. They were Governor Sharpe of Maryland (the builder of Whitehall), Governor Shirley of Massachusetts (the builder of Shirley Place), and the Governors of Virginia, Pennsylvania, and New York. Carlyle House was the headquarters of General Braddock, and the purpose of this meeting was to discuss the strategy and logistics of the French and

Carlyle House, Alexandria, Virginia. The house, which dates from 1752, is being restored,
but the flankers have long since gone.

Indian War. The Stamp Act was one of the proposals made for financing the campaign, and its
later enactment sowed the seeds of rebellion that eventually led to the War of Independence.

Carlyle House was built in 1752 by John Carlyle, a native of Scotland who had married a
cousin of Lord Fairfax, the owner of one-fifth of what is now the Commonwealth of Virginia.
Colonel Carlyle was one of the original incorporators of Alexandria, and in 1750 chose the best
site in the new town for his house, with magnificent views across the Potomac from the terrace at
the back. The house had attendant pavilions, not attached to the main block, and a large forecourt.
The walls were of brick, framed by quoins of rusticated limestone. The design is borrowed from
Vitruvius Scoticus, which contained smaller houses than the *Britannicus*, more easily adapted to
life in the colonies. In this particular case, it could have been for sentimental reasons that Carlyle
chose a Scottish model. The design comes from Craigiehall House, West Lothian (c. 1725), Plate
LXXXVII, but no details of its construction are known as the family records were destroyed at the
time of the War Between the States.

The central block of Carlyle House was erected about seventy-five feet back from Fairfax
Street, with the advanced flankers placed approximately on the present building line. It is believed
that there were no connecting walls or arcades built, although they may have been planned. The
illustration shows the house after it had been remodeled in the Federal style in the nineteenth
century. The roof was raised to provide a third story, the entrance door changed, and various interior

A Pendleton lithograph of Mount Airy.

Mount Airy, Warsaw, Virginia, built by Colonel John Tayloe II in 1758, has remained in the family to the present day.

alterations carried out. For a hundred and thirty-three years Alexandria's grandest house was hidden behind a hotel erected between it and Fairfax Street. It is now owned by the Virginia Regional Park Authority, which has exposed it to view once more and has restored it as part of a planned historical park.

Plate LVI in *Vitruvius Scoticus* illustrates Haddo House, erected c. 1725 for Lord Aberdeen. Building at Mount Airy, near Warsaw, Virginia, must have been under way shortly after William Adam's designs were published in 1750, as it was finished by 1758 when Colonel John Tayloe II wrote that he had completed "in ten years" the houses, outbuildings, and landscaping. This undoubtedly included a considerable amount of earthwork that had to be done before building could start. *Vitruvius Scoticus* furnished the inspiration for the entrance front, based on the central section of Haddo House, with details borrowed from Newliston and The Drum.

Mount Airy, which stands on a rise overlooking the river five miles distant, is the first complete Palladian scheme in America, having a central block connected to advance buildings by quadrant passages. It is built of a local dark brown sandstone, laid in random coursing, and trimmed with Portland and local Aquia Creek stone. The central motif, as at Haddo, has three windows beneath a pediment. Here, however, the entrance is different; there is a loggia with square piers as at Newliston. In the center of the east front there is a large Palladian window, similar in detail to

The south front of Mount Airy, looking to the river.

The entrance hall of Mount Airy.

The dining room of Mount Airy. The mantel is one of those installed in the house after the fire.

Road coach arriving for a luncheon at Mount Airy, 1974.

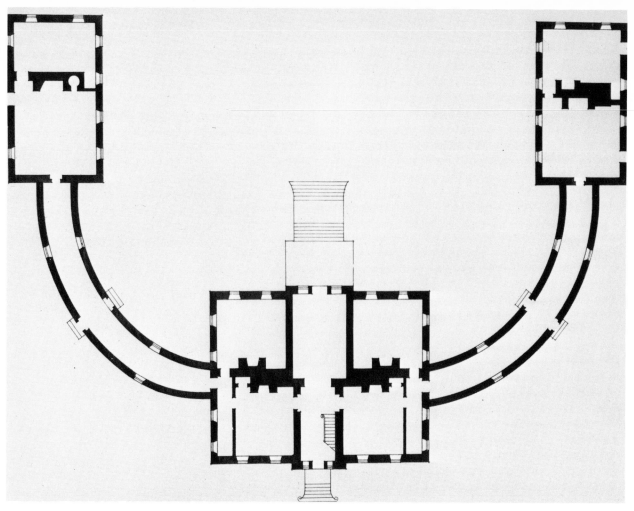

The plan of Mannsfield was modeled on Mount Airy.

those on the connecting links at The Drum. The south front, which faces the Rappahannock River, is taken from *A Book of Architecture* by James Gibbs, published in 1728. Plate 58, "A design Made for a Gentleman in Dorsetshire," also has a loggia with three arches as its central motif. There is a stringcourse above the keystones crowned by a pediment, as at Saraceno, but Gibbs has introduced three windows rather than one; at Mount Airy the stringcourse continues around all four sides of the house.

Originally two subsidiary buildings, one of which survives, added to the breadth of the composition in true Palladian fashion. They were connected by fences and gates forming utilitarian yards to either side, as shown in the Pendleton lithograph. In the garden there is an orangery, now in ruins, and farther away the racetrack and stables that once housed such famous Thoroughbreds as Tychicus, Yorick, and Sir Archie.

The entrance court is reached by a flight of molded Portland stone steps between pedestals supporting elaborately carved stone urns. Another flight, now guarded by great stone dogs, leads to the north entrance loggia. This has pilastered piers supporting a full stone entablature with square niches to either side. The great hall door is not original; it was replaced after a disastrous fire that gutted the interior and destroyed the roof. The new roof is a simple hip, in place of hip-on-hip that was originally surmounted by a carved pineapple as at Brandon and Battersea.

The great hall running through the house had a marble floor, but after the fire this was replaced by a William Van Ness pine floor with a compass, inlaid in contrasting woods, in the center. The interior was probably "Gibbs's Modern," of the type that still exists at Kenmore as referred to in John Ariss's advertisement:

110

Mannsfield (c. 1760), Fredericksburg, Virginia, was built by a Miss Tayloe of Mount Airy and her husband, Mann Page II.

By the Subscriber (lately from GREAT BRITAIN), Buildings of all Sorts and Dimensions are undertaken and performed in the neatest Manner, (and at the cheapest Rates), either of the Ancient or Modern Order of *Gibbs*'s Architect, and if any Gentleman should want Plans, Bills of Scantling, or Bills of Charges, for any Fabric, or Public Edifice, may have them by applying to the Subscriber at Major *John Bushrod*'s, at *Westmoreland* County, *Virginia*, where may be seen a great Variety, and sundry Draughts of Buildings in Miniature, and also some Buildings near finished, after the Modern Taste. JOHN ARISS.

Ariss lived in the adjoining county and could have been the bearer of *Vitruvius Scoticus* and *A Book of Architecture*. John Tayloe was educated in England; he may well have explored the English country houses and determined to build one for himself. In 1740 he acquired the land, and eight years later began to prepare the chosen site for building. By the time John Ariss arrived in the country, all was ready for work to begin, and Ariss is the most likely candidate for the design. William Buckland came to Richmond County before 1762, possibly to work for Ariss who had lately moved there, and it would appear that he worked on some of the finishing touches at Mount Airy. John Tayloe, writing to his neighbor at Sabine Hall on October 16, 1762, concludes: ". . . and if you would ride to Mt. Airy sometimes and give your friendly hints of admonition to Mr. Buckland I believe it would be doing me no small service." The office that survived the fire unscathed contained a wooden cornice that was used in restoring the mantels in the library and dining room. Similar in detail to Buckland's work at Gunston Hall, this carving is convincing evidence that he worked at Mount Airy before moving on to Annapolis.

Blandfield (c. 1770), Caret, Virginia, built by William Beverley, who married another of Colonel Tayloe's daughters.

One of John Tayloe's daughters married Mann Page II, who had inherited Rosewell, the largest mansion in Colonial Virginia. Making it over to his eldest son, Page began the building of Mannsfield, another of the great houses of the Rappahannock. As at Mount Airy, there was a main block connected to two advance buildings by quadrant passages. The long axes of these dependencies faced the approach, creating a deeper forecourt. Built of stone, the house was described by Latrobe in 1796 as "in the style of the Country Gentleman's house in England of 50 years ago." Mannsfield passed out of the Page family and was destroyed in 1862.

Blandfield is yet a third Rappahannock mansion. It was built by William Beverley, who married a sister of Mrs. Mann Page; the plantation is still owned by their descendants. It is of brick rather than stone; the advance buildings are joined to the house by straight passages. Having retained its original roof, Blandfield shows best the original feeling of these three houses. Although the exterior is unchanged, the interior as finished by William Beverley was altered in the nineteenth century. After the interiors at Mount Airy were simplified, following the fire of 1844, the owner of Blandfield ripped out the gray marble mantels and the fashionable papers and borders installed by the original owner in 1771 and replaced them with the severest of plain painted work. It is said that this is the only fire to have gutted two houses.

"Amongst the uppermost circles in Philadelphia," wrote Samuel Weld in 1795, "pride, haughtiness and ostentation are conspicuous; and it seems as if nothing could make them happier than that an order of nobility should be established." If such sentiments accord ill with the principles of William Penn, they may be thanked for the fine houses built by prosperous Philadelphians in

112

The entrance front of Mount Pleasant, Fairmount Park, Philadelphia, built in 1761 for
Captain John MacPherson.

The parlor of Mount Pleasant.

The great chamber of Mount Pleasant.

Cliveden (1764), Germantown, Pennsylvania, built by Benjamin Chew. Samuel Chew presented the house and its contents to the National Trust for Historic Preservation in 1972.

what is now Fairmount Park, on the northern edge of the city. Like the villas on the Thames near London, or the marine residences on the outskirts of Dublin, these were near enough to the city for business to be transacted during the day and country air enjoyed at night. The city's water supply comes from here, and, for fear of polluting it, no further building has been permitted over the years. The miniature estates have survived, their houses restored and furnished by the Philadelphia Museum of Art. Nine of them are regularly open to the public, and eight more may be seen by special application to the Museum.

Mount Pleasant is the finest of these houses. It was built for Captain John MacPherson, a Scottish privateer and inventor, in 1761. The plan is interesting; a long axial hallway of generous proportions leads right through the house from front to back. This arrangement is repeated on the bedroom floor, so as to provide ventilation in hot weather. On each side of the entrance drive is a balancing barn, as well as the twin service buildings illustrated here. Nothing is known of the architect, but the chaste Palladian style might well have appealed to an immigrant Scot in a nest of Quakers, and it would be natural for a sea captain to crown his house with a widow's walk. Philadelphia furniture of the period is on display here, shown off to perfection in the period rooms with their ornamental carving.

Cliveden, near Philadelphia, has now passed into the care of the National Trust, and the house was opened to the public for the first time in 1972. Except for a break of eighteen years, it had remained in the Chew family since it was built in 1763. Such continuity is unusual, and

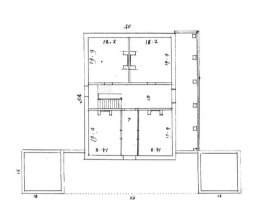

A study for Cliveden from the hand of Benjamin Chew.

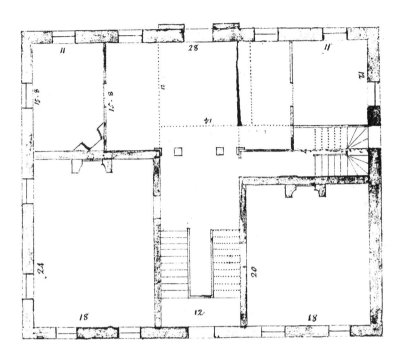

Final study for the floor plan, by Chew.

Kew Palace, London, from an engraving published in the *Gentleman's Magazine,* 1763.

115

This further study for Cliveden is close to the design of the house as built, apart from the front door.

The entrance hall of Cliveden.

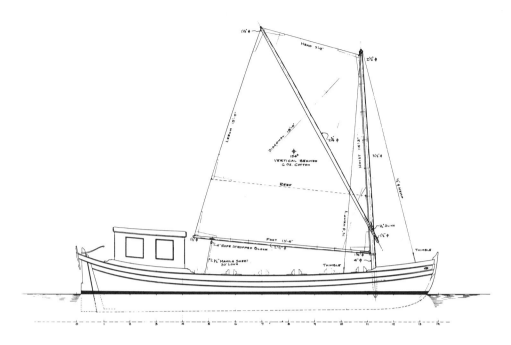

This craft, modeled after the Thames barges, is a reproduction of that belonging to William Penn. Governor Sharpe had a similar vessel at his disposal.

especially valuable is the very complete set of documents relating to the building of the house and its furnishing, which has remained here. The total absence of factual information in houses like Mount Pleasant makes such documentation especially useful.

Attorney General Benjamin Chew bought eleven acres of land in Germantown, Pennsylvania, in 1763, and eventually came to own sixty. He sketched out the house he wanted, and alternative plans were drawn up for him. Among these drawings in the Chew papers is an engraving of the palace at Kew, a Palladian design which evidently inspired the outline of the house. Another plan shows three blocks linked by arches, each showing a pediment to the front. In the final result it was modified to a single block of five bays, built of a golden-brown sandstone with gray limestone dressings, and surmounted by a pediment. Behind the house a pair of pedimented flankers recall the original tripartite scheme.

Five stone urns, which Chew had shipped from Bristol, ornament the parapet and pediment. He wrote, on December 12, 1766:

> I have shown the pattern of the urns sent over by Mr. Pennington to the knowing ones among us and have fixed on No. 2 only that it is to have little or no carve work as most suitable to the plainness of my building. I shall be much obliged to you therefore to forward the enclosed by the ship now sailing for London [to] Pennington & press him to use his kind endeavors [to have] them finish'd as soon as possible and sent over early in the spring when I shall want to set them up.

The Battle of Germantown in October 1777 raged around Cliveden, and the house and grounds emerged bruised and shaken by shells and bullets. The battle scars can be seen to this day. The bill for urns mentions seven, but only five are ever shown to decorate the house, even on the earliest drawing. The other two may have suffered on the voyage, or have been the garden "vases" mentioned as being damaged at the time of the battle.

The wide hall of Cliveden possibly served as the principal reception room, for there is no other approaching it in size. Much of the ground floor is taken up with this generous space. It would be interesting to know if it was used as the "pivot of the house," for living in, or kept empty as a front hall should be.

The Whitehall main doors, front and back, are identical.

Detail of the carved woodwork, which is attributed to William Buckland.

The entrance front of Whitehall.

The Chew papers, of which Margaret Tinkcom has made an excellent study, contain an exhaustive list of all the materials used in building the house. There is not a yard of cornice, a shutter, floorboard, rope, chain, or carved pilaster unaccounted for. Among other things, the papers reveal that building a house was thirsty work. Fourteen and three-quarter barrels and three casks of beer lasted only from April to November of 1765, and six gallons of rum were consumed in October of that year. In making the future of Cliveden secure, the National Trust is preserving a family tradition, furniture and pictures of importance, and muniments that reveal in detail the divers problems of building a house in the 1760s.

Colonel Horatio Sharpe, erstwhile Commander in Chief of His Majesty's forces in Virginia, was appointed Governor of Maryland in 1753. As there was no official residence, he rented a house in Annapolis, and ten years later purchased a large tract of land opposite the town at the mouth of the Severn River, on which he erected a pavilion for entertaining. It is a distant cousin of the Banqueting Houses at Hall Barn and Studley Royal in England, and the Marino Casino in Ireland; such buildings frequently overlooked water and provided elegant shelter during daytime expeditions. Whitehall was approached by water. A governor's barge was quite an elaborate affair, twenty-seven or more feet in length, with colored sails and gilded cushions. Governor Sharpe's barge was rowed by eight single oarsmen and steered by the boatswain in charge; there was a cabin for passengers near the stern. All important traffic went, where possible, by water. At the head of the lawn visitors to Whitehall were greeted by the sight of the first temple-form dwelling in the New World and entered a great portico which dominates the façade. It is hewn from solid tree trunks, and the fluted Corinthian columns are set upon molded brick bases. The capitals and entablature are superbly carved, and each dentil and modillion on the architrave and cornice is

119

Whitehall, Annapolis, Maryland. The river front. The house was built in 1765 by Governor Sharpe as a pavilion for entertaining.

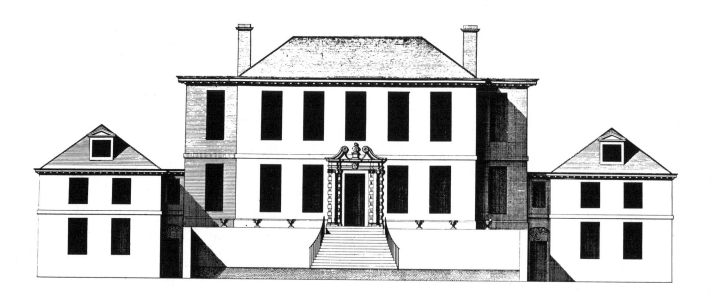

Plate 49 from *Vitruvius Britannicus,* "Front of Mr. Rooth's House at Epsom."

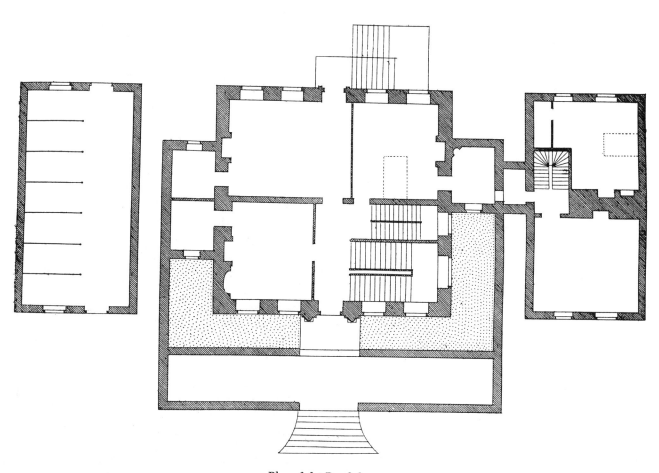

Plan of the Rooth house.

Shirley, Charles City County, Virginia, built by the Hill–Carters and still in their possession.

decorated. This splendid entrance opens into the great hall which occupies the entire central block, its tray ceiling extending into the roof space. This is a smaller yet more elaborately decorated version of the great hall at Stratford Hall, Virginia. There was only one room on either side of the hall— a ladies' parlor and a smoking room for the gentlemen.

The woodwork for the interior of Whitehall may have been executed by William Buckland, although he did not establish a permanent residence in Annapolis until 1771. Governor Sharpe is known to have visited George Mason at Gunston Hall and may very well have been acquainted with Buckland. From 1762 until he moved to Maryland, Buckland lived in the Northern Neck of Virginia, working in the vicinity, and he frequently made the three days' journey to Annapolis. In about the year 1765 there were no less than seven great houses being built in this neighborhood, all with similar characteristics.

The original plans for Whitehall called for an impressive length of 258 feet, but the extremities, which would have included bathrooms with running water, were apparently never built. However, upon Sharpe's retirement in 1769, he did extend the house to make it livable all the year round. Work on the building continued until 1773 when Sharpe made a journey to England to visit his brothers; the outbreak of the Revolution prevented his return. When he died, the property was inherited by his secretary, John Ridout, who had cared for it in Sharpe's absence. It was the Ridout summer home for more than a hundred years. The wings were further extended during this period, and a second story added to the two side rooms. In contrast to the vicissitudes

Shirley: the flying staircase.

The drawing room of Shirley was the entrance chamber for visitors approaching by water.

The dining room of Shirley.

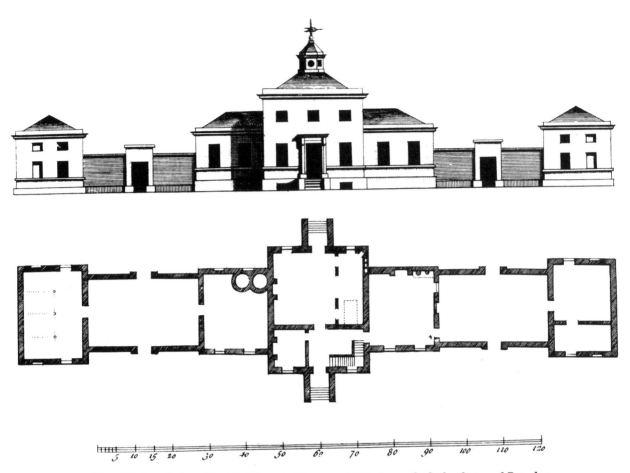

Plate III from Robert Morris's *Select Architecture*, 1757, from which the design of Brandon was taken.

borne by Tazewell Hall, the great hall of Whitehall has remained throughout the years as Governor Sharpe left it. The present owners, Mr. and Mrs. Charles Scarlett, Jr., have removed the second-floor rooms, and the house has returned to its original temple form.

Buckland's connection with the building is still not fully authenticated, although the interior detailing is close to some of his known work. According to Beirne and Scarff, "The strongest motive for crediting him with the woodwork of Whitehall is the fact that no other man of the period capable of executing the design is known."

Shirley Plantation, Charles City County, Virginia, has remained in one family for more than three hundred years, since Edward Hill patented nine thousand acres here in 1660. He kept the name given to the property earlier in the century by Lord Delaware, whose wife's maiden name it was. Elizabeth Hill, Edward's great-granddaughter, inherited the property. In 1723 she married John Carter of Corotoman, son of Robert, known as "King" Carter because the land he owned was measured in square miles rather than acres. This established the Hill-Carter line, which has remained at Shirley until today. The present generation continues to live at Shirley and also shares it with the general public.

There has been some disagreement as to which generation of Carters built the present house. The most likely candidate is John Hill Carter, who married the heiress Elizabeth in 1723 and died in 1742. There is mention of a bricklayer and masons working here in 1738 and 1739, probably on the outbuildings. There is also a sketch showing what purports to be the seventeenth-century house (demolished in 1868) standing in the way of the elegant approach to the house

124

Brandon, Prince George County, Virginia, was completed in 1765 for Nathaniel Harrison.

Battersea, Petersburg, Virginia, in an early photograph. The five-part composition may derive from Brandon, a few miles downriver. A wooden three-part version of Battersea, Strawberry Hill, now undergoing restoration, stands nearby.

The staircase of Battersea.

The Old Exchange, Charleston. Now a museum, the building was erected by the German architects Peter and John Horlbeck in 1767. Detail of a painting by Thomas Leitch (Leech) titled "View of Charlestown, 1774."

through the two pairs of forecourt buildings. The house and outbuildings were obviously conceived at one time. Thomas Waterman considered that it was built by Charles Hill Carter after his mother Elizabeth's death in 1769.

Everything about Shirley seems to indicate the earlier period: the steep pitch of the roof, the dormer windows, tall chimneys, and the four-pane sashes flush with the brickwork. Inside, the paneled walls, baroque overdoors, and massive fireplace projections are features normally associated with the first half of the eighteenth century. The very formality of the approach to the house through the sentry-like outbuildings confirms this impression.

It is the double-tiered porches on either façade that are Palladian, handsome porticoes that were added to the house in 1831, a hundred years after it was built. Beneath the granite paving are the old steps of the more modest porch that was original to the house. This was the river entrance of Shirley and therefore the main front door. The plan of the house and the original stoop was taken from Volume II, Plate 48, of Campbell's *Vitruvius Britannicus*, a copy of which was in the library at Westover, the neighboring plantation of William Byrd II.

At Gunston Hall an up-to-date interior is concealed behind an early façade. At Shirley the opposite is the case—a Queen Anne façade hides behind a classical portico. It is a tribute to the

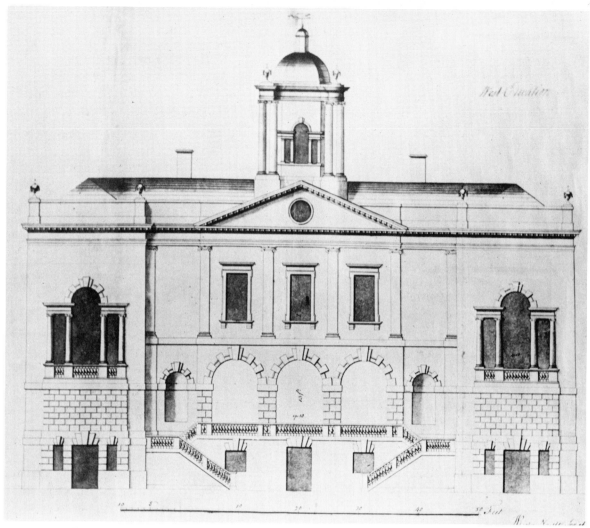

Drawing of the west elevation of the Old Exchange signed by William Rigby Naylor, an employee of Thomas Wooden.

Carters that these elements should combine in so satisfactory a manner. The architectural purists who attempt to stick rigidly to a particular date when restoring a house might learn something from Shirley. An old house, and preserved with care, it has been spared the uniform look that is sometimes left by the Williamsburg embalmers.

Brandon, on the James River, is a five-part house where the wings were built first. It has been suggested that the central block was designed by Jefferson, whose architectural talents were always available to his friends. Nathaniel Harrison, the owner, completed the house at the time of his marriage in 1765.

Battersea, near Petersburg, is a house of the same type, with the wings joined by one-story hyphens to a central block. The Marquis de Chastellux visited Battersea in 1780 and described it as being "decorated rather than in the Italian style." It contains a fine Chinese Chippendale staircase.

The Old Exchange in Charleston, maintained as a museum by the Daughters of the American Revolution, closes the end of Broad Street in a suitably dignified manner. It is a provincial essay in Palladianism; the builders seem to have been uncertain about the level of the windows

Miles Brewton House, Charleston, built in 1765 to the designs of Ezra Waite, an Englishman.

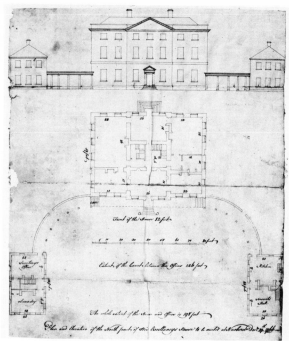

Plan and elevation of Tryon Palace, New Bern, North Carolina, by the English architect John Hawks, dated 1766.

The drawing room takes up most of the upper level of the Miles Brewton House on the front facing the street.

as between the front and sides, resulting in a peculiar compromise with the stringcourse. The author of the design is not known, but the contractors were two German immigrants named Peter and John Horlbeck, who had arrived in Charleston in 1764. The following announcement appeared in the *South Carolina Gazette:*

Charles-Town, Sept. 9, 1767

Notice is hereby given, to any person or persons, who are willing to undertake the building of the intended Exchange in Charles Town, and to furnish materials for the same, agreeable to a plan thereof, which is to be seen in the hands of the subscriber; that they do give in their proposals, on or before the first day of October next, to

Tho. Farr, jun.

The Horlbecks won the contract and were voted £40,936 on condition that the building be finished by January 1771. Detailed specifications accompanied the plan, for instance:

Two Venetian Windows to the Stair Cases of the intire Ionick Order. . . . Four Columns and Twenty-four Pilasters of the Ionick Order. . . . Twelve Arches. . . . The Covering of the Roof to be of Welch Carnavan Slate. The Roof of the Cupelo and the Bed of the Entablature to be covered with Lead. . . . All the rooms and Passages to be Wainscotted Chair high with proper Base and Sur Base, Eight Folding Doors to one of Stairs . . . . and Folding Doors to the two Stair Cases, Double Architraves to the same. The Large Room Wainscotted Fourteen feet high with eight Columns and twenty

Tryon Palace, originally built in 1767. All but the stable block was destroyed; rebuilding began in 1952.

The front hall of Tryon Palace.

Pilasters and Entablature of three feet high of the Ionic Order, a Cove Ceiling to the same six feet high, two neat Chimney Pieces and Pediment to the Doors, sixteen square windows and two Blank Windows.

The "Large Room" was the ballroom in which, having addressed the populace from the front of the Old Exchange in 1791, George Washington admired "256 elegantly dressed and handsome ladies." It was not the only interesting feature of the building. Facing the sea was a formal entrance for those arriving by water, "who upon passing through the open arcade under the Great Hall would emerge upon a perspective as compelling as any designed by Palladio." Roberts Mills, the high priest of the Greek Revival, wrote of it in 1826. "Though its style of architecture is not what we desire to see imitated, yet it is a fine building and shows in its construction how faithfully public work was executed in 'the olden time.' " To him the building already seemed antiquated.

It is satisfying to learn that the stone urns and the cupola are soon to be replaced, and that everything possible will be done to put the building back as it was in 1771. This worthy undertaking has been endorsed by the Mayor of Charleston, and will further enhance the city, already richer in old buildings than any other in the New World.

Drayton Hall is the finest country house of the Charleston area, and the Miles Brewton House is its equivalent in town. They resemble one another—both are Palladian villas, built of brick, with a white double portico on the front. The portico at the Miles Brewton House has Ionic columns of wood above Doric columns of Portland stone. It projects to form a veranda above and

Plan of Monticello.

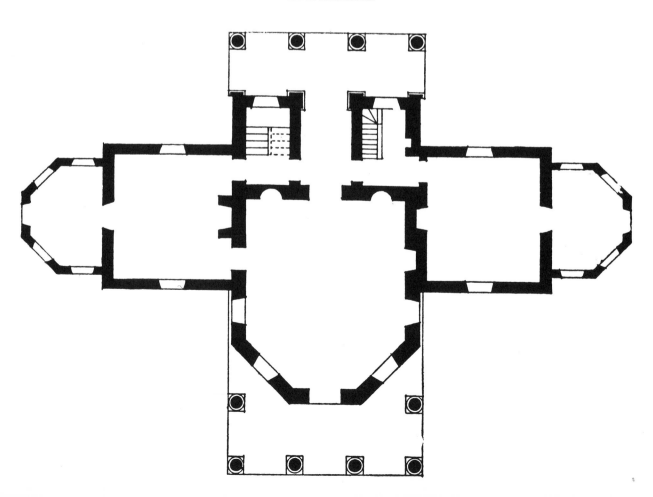

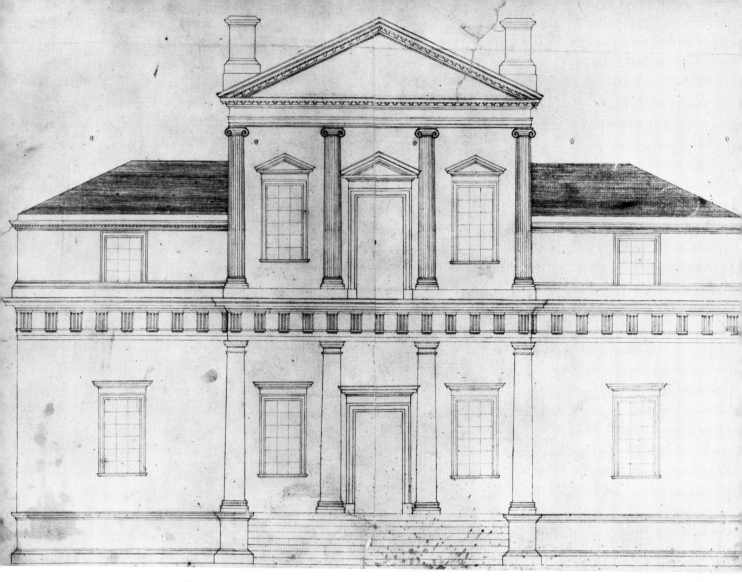

Monticello, Charlottesville, Virginia. This is the 1769 house as originally designed for himself by Thomas Jefferson. He later remodeled it to its present form.

provide shade and shelter to the front door. Shade is all-important in Charleston, where the heat of summer used to drive all who could afford it to the North Carolina mountains or even as far as Newport. The climate influenced the design of the typical Charleston house, built with one end to the street, and a colonnade or piazza running along the side, facing the yard or garden. The great portico at the Miles Brewton House faces east down Ladson-Street and was built more for show than for sitting. It achieves its striking effect from subtle gradations of height, being set at the top of a double staircase with a central rusticated door leading into the basement below. Full view of this great portico is afforded the pedestrian through elegantly wrought iron gates linked to stone piers by railings. Curved curtain walls lead to flanking piers, made of a buff-colored stone to match the front steps. The whole composition is generously balanced, and the white columns, red brick, buff stone, and black ironwork combine in perfect harmony. Add the dark green of magnolia leaves and the blue sky and it is easy to see why this has been described as the most beautiful town house in America.

The house was built from 1765 to 1769 by Ezra Waite, who advertised his services as "civil architect, Housebuilder in general and Carver from London." Waite stated that he "finished the Architecture, conducted the . . . said work in the four principal rooms; and also calculated, adjusted, and draw'd . . . the Ionick entablature, and carved the same on the front and around the eaves." The Doric Portland stone columns are not mentioned, because they were imported

Lansdowne, Fairmount Park, Philadelphia, built for Governor John Penn by an unknown architect in 1773. Engraving by W. Birch.

The Lansdowne portrait of George Washington by Gilbert Stuart.

Drawing by Charles Bulfinch of Senator William Bingham's town house on Third Street, Philadelphia, which influenced Bulfinch's design for the first Harrison Gray Otis house on Cambridge Street in Boston.

already carved, as were the marble mantels. Two of the downstairs rooms have identical mantels which may originally have been destined for the great drawing room above; a room of this size in England might easily have had twin mantels. The drawing room takes up most of the front of the house. The mantel, probably imported and dwarfed by the seventeen-foot ceiling, has been given an elaborate overmantel with a scroll pediment to bring it into scale with the room. The intricately carved cornice is of wood, not plaster, and is surmounted by bold coving. The doorcases have straight broken pediments supported by Corinthian pilasters, and the windows have shouldered surrounds. The carving on the mahogany staircase is of superb quality, and Waite must have had a competent team working under him. There is evidence that he possessed Chippendale's *Director*, for Chinese and Gothic are mixed with rococo detail. The influence of this *vade mecum* can be seen in the front court wall and the gothick stable, as shown in *The Only Proper Style* by Calder Loth and Julius Trousdale Sadler, Jr. The Miles Brewton house has come to Mr. and Mrs. Edward Manigault by descent, and some of the furniture and pictures have remained here since the time it was built.

Tryon Palace, New Bern, North Carolina, has had two lives. It was originally built in 1767 to the designs of John Hawks (1731–1790), an English architect who had worked under Stiff Leadbetter at Nuneham Courtenay, Oxfordshire. He came over to America with William Tryon,

Portrait by Charles Willson Peale of William Buckland begun in 1774, the year of the architect's death, and completed in 1789.

who was appointed Governor of the Colony in 1765. Perhaps as a means of ensuring that the necessary funds would be voted for such an elaborate residence, the main apartment on the ground floor was given over to the Council Room. A plan dated 1766 at the New-York Historical Society shows a three-story central block and three-bay wings; in execution the top floor was lost, but the wings were made wider by one bay.

The final plan, dated 1767, was sent over to England "for His Majesty's approbation" and is in the Public Record Office in London. In front of the house there is a spacious forecourt with kitchen block on the left and stables on the right. The risk of fire may have been the incentive for keeping the kitchen away from the main house (see plan, page 130), but to have it so far from the dining room can hardly have been convenient. Tryon imported not only his architect from England but also his mantels. He describes one of them in detail in a letter to Lord Hillsborough: "A large statuary Ionic chimney piece, the shafts of the columns sienna and the frett on the Frieze inlaid with the same. A rich edge and foliage on the Tablet, medals of the King and Queen on the Frieze over the Columns, the Mouldings enriched, a large statuary marble slab and black marble coverings."

The capital of North Carolina moved to Raleigh in 1794, and three years later the main part of the palace burned to the ground. Subsequently new houses and roads covered the grounds. The legendary magnificence of the palace lingered on, however, in the minds of the people of New Bern. The existence of an inventory, plans, and contemporary descriptions of Tryon made possible the recreation of the palace, which by 1950 had vanished without trace. True, the west wing still stood, but it was unrecognizable as such, having been plastered over and further disguised by a new roof, chimneys, and porch.

Determined Tryon Palace should come to life again, the late Mrs. James Latham, her daughter, Mrs. John Kellenberger, Miss Gertrude Carraway, and others provided the necessary

The garden front of Hammond–Harwood House.

Hammond–Harwood House (1774), Annapolis, Maryland, designed by William Buckland. ". . . superb houses that would not disgrace Westminster, Col. Ed. Lloyd, Mr. Hammond. . . ." (From the 1787 diary of Samuel Vaughan, English friend of George Washington.)

The dining room of Hammond–Harwood House, showing a false door introduced for balance.

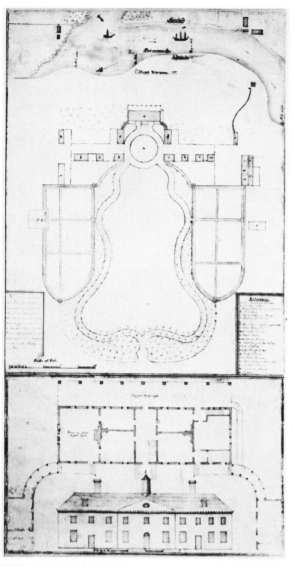

The plan, elevation, and garden layout of Mount Vernon, as drawn in 1787 by Samuel Vaughan. It is the earliest surviving ground plan of Mount Vernon.

The river front of Mount Vernon, Fairfax County, Virginia, taken from C. W. Janson's *The Stranger in America,* published in 1807.

The Venetian window in the banquet hall of Mount Vernon, visible in Janson's watercolor. The plasterwork was completed in 1786.

funds and expertise, and in 1952 excavation of the site began. The old foundations were revealed, and the colors found on scraps of plaster in the rubble helped decide the decoration of the interior. Pieces of marble flooring, moldings, and brass hardware from the burned windows and doors were carefully examined. William Perry was the architect in charge of the rebuilding and the exhaustive research that was necessary. The project eventually involved the re-siting of two roads. Like the phoenix, Tryon Palace rose again from its own ashes. Today it attracts visitors from far and wide as a living example of the elegance of pre-Revolutionary America.

Thomas Jefferson built himself a new house, Monticello, astride a hilltop near Shadwell, his old family home in Virginia. He began leveling the site in 1768. "How sublime," he wrote, "to look down into the workhouse of nature, to see her clouds, hail, snow, thunder all fabricated at our feet and the glorious sun when rising as out of a distant water, just gilding the top of the mountains." Architecture was his passion, and were it not for his own drawings and for two contemporary accounts, the early Monticello would have vanished without a trace. Jefferson could not resist improving and changing the house, and admitted: "Architecture is my delight, and putting up and

Parts of the Wye House orangery may be earlier than the house.

Wye House, Talbot County, Maryland, built in 1784 for Edward Lloyd, whose family has been seated here since 1623.

Hampton, Towson, Maryland, built in 1783 for Charles Ridgely. The architect is not known. There are few known examples of a portico with closed ends.

pulling down one of my favorite amusements." The plan of the first Monticello was taken from Morris's *Select Architecture*, and the elevation is adapted from Palladio. The upper room was Jefferson's library—here he could shut himself away with his books, or look out between the columns at the monumental view.

The buildings he admired during his tour of duty as minister and then ambassador in Paris gave him fresh ideas. On his return he removed the top story of Monticello and transformed his Palladian villa into the neoclassical house that is there to the present day, inspired by the pavilion-type houses he had seen abroad.

On December 12, 1780, in his *Travels in North America*, the Marquis de Chastellux wrote: "The beautiful banks of the Schuylkill are everywhere covered with beautiful country houses; amongst others, those of Mr. Penn, the late proprietor, and Mr. Peters, late Secretary to the Board of War, are on the most delightful situations." Mr. Peters's "tasty little box," Belmont, still survives in West Fairmount Park, Philadelphia, adjoining the land where Lansdowne stood.

The building of Lansdowne was started in 1773 by Deputy Governor John Penn, grandson of the founder, on two hundred acres across the Schuylkill from the family manor of Sprigettsbury, on a bluff above the river. The house was built in the Italian style, a new departure for the time and place, at the end of a long driveway lined with catalpa trees. The double portico made its appearance here for the first time in the Northern colonies. A contemporary described the columns

as Ionic; there were quoins at the corners, and a widow's walk; urns and statues decorated the grounds. After Penn's death in 1795, the house was seized from the new owner in a bankruptcy action and purchased by Senator William Bingham in 1797 for the impressive sum of $55,000.

Senator Bingham had made a fortune in Martinique. Returning to Philadelphia, he married in 1780, and he and his bride paid a lengthy visit to Europe. When they came back to Philadelphia after five years abroad, it was to build, on Third Street, a larger and more pretentious version of Manchester House, London. Bingham could well afford this extravagance, for he was the richest man in the country, owning four million acres of land in Pennsylvania, New York, and Maine. Charles Bulfinch, the Boston architect, made a drawing of the house when he was in Philadelphia in 1789, and wrote: "The house of Mr. Bingham . . . is in a stile that would be esteemed splendid even in the most luxurious parts of Europe. Elegance of construction, white marble staircase, valuable paintings, the richest furniture and the utmost magnificence of decoration makes it a palace in my opinion far too rich for any man in this country."

Annfield, Berryville, Virginia, built for Mathew Page in 1790, displays a fine rural example of a double portico.

Gilbert Stuart was commissioned to paint a full-length portrait of George Washington at his Germantown studio. The President wrote to Stuart on April 11, 1796: "I am under promise to Mrs. Bingham to sit for you tomorrow, at nine o'clock." A replica was ordered which was presented to the Earl of Shelburne, later the Marquis of Lansdowne, who had acted as a strong defender of the Colonies in Parliament. Senator Bingham hung the portrait at Lansdowne House, and on his death in 1804 it passed to the Pennsylvania Academy of the Fine Arts.

For a time Lansdowne stood empty, save for occasional short leaseholds. It briefly regained some of its former splendor when tenanted by Joseph Bonaparte, the dethroned King of Spain. On

Federal Hall, New York City, was built in 1788 to the designs of Pierre L'Enfant in time for Washington's inauguration as first President of the United States in the following year. (From the engraving by Amos Doolittle.)

July 4, 1854, it was burned out in a blaze started by fireworks set off within the grounds. In 1865 the walls were pulled down, and the land was acquired in 1866 from the Baring family in England by the City of Philadelphia and became a part of Fairmount Park. In 1876 the Centennial Exposition was held on the property, and Memorial Hall occupies the site where Lansdowne House once stood.

The portrait of William Buckland, started in the spring of 1774 by Charles Willson Peale, displays symbols of his profession; there is a column and a classical portico in the background, and on the table are drawing instruments with the plan and elevation of the house he was then building for Matthias Hammond. Hammond, a young lawyer, had commissioned the house when he became engaged, and it is Buckland's crowning—and final—achievement, for he died that winter before it was completed.

The house stands across the street from the Chase–Lloyd house, which Buckland also had a hand in, although it was begun by a "supervising builder" from England. Elizabeth Lloyd, wife of the new owner, grew up at Mount Airy, where Buckland had worked some years before. The Chase–Lloyd house is a square town house of three stories. Documents show that Buckland started on the Hammond house as work on the Chase–Lloyd house was drawing to a close; they complement each other across the brick-paved street. The Hammond house is built in vermilion brick laid in Flemish bond, and relies for its effect on elegant proportions and on such details as the doorways, the window trim above them, and the arched window that lights the stairs. Three-sided bays are used here for the first time in the thirteen colonies.

Elaborate interior woodwork enlivens Buckland's masterpiece. There is a contrast between the simplicity of the hall and the ornamentation of the adjoining dining room with its lively carved

The White House, Washington, D.C., designed by the Irish architect James Hoban, who won the competition of 1792. Shown is the north portico, added by Benjamin Latrobe in 1829.

144

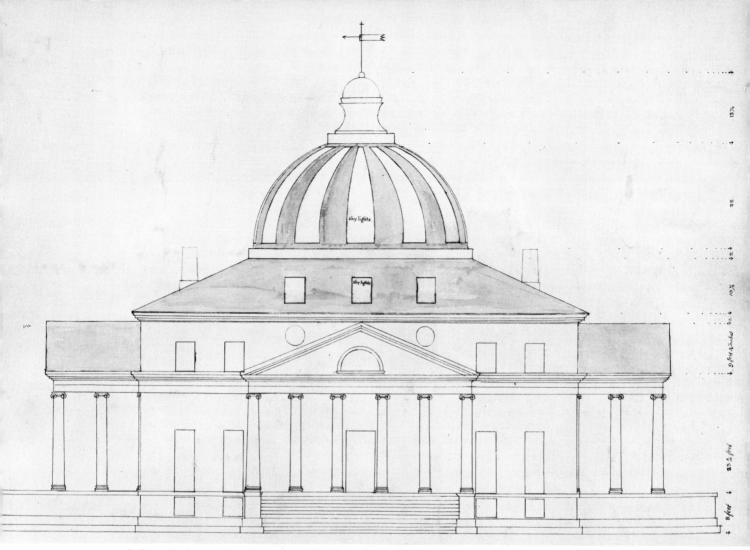

Jefferson's design, based on the Villa Rotonda, with which he entered the President's Palace competition.

overmantel. The entablatures of the doors and windows have carved friezes, the shutters have octagonal panels, and a rich cornice crowns the whole. Every room in the house has a carved mantel, each one to a different design. They are all mid-Georgian in style, apart from the upstairs ballroom, which perhaps was unfinished at the time of Buckland's death and is, as a result, more restrained. There is no carving over doors or chimney breast; ornament is confined to Adamesque urns in the frieze, oval rosettes, knots of ribbon, and a garland of roses on the mantel.

Matthias Hammond never moved into the house. His fiancée eloped with another man, and Hammond went to live on one of his plantations, leaving the Annapolis house untenanted until his death in 1786. Thomas Jefferson attended the Continental Congress here in 1783 and 1784, and the house so intrigued him that he took the time to measure it. The drawing he made is in the Coolidge Collection. The nephew who inherited the property promptly sold it, after which it passed through many hands. Lafayette was entertained here in 1824. A later owner, Richard Harwood, whose name is still attached to the house, married the architect's granddaughter. She brought the Peale portrait to hang in the elegant surroundings created by William Buckland, and an excellent copy by Winifred Gordon hangs in the ballroom today. The house was purchased at auction by St. John's College in 1926 and briefly opened as a house museum. The Hammond–Harwood House Association reopened it in 1938 for the display of their collection of Maryland eighteenth-century furniture and portraits; it is now open to the public every day except Christmas.

Mount Vernon, George Washington's estate on the banks of the Potomac, had been in his family since 1694, and he lies buried in the family vault on the grounds. The entrance front of the

145

The west end of the White House with its Venetian window and giant pilasters. Drawing by W. Blodgett.

The south front of the White House, showing the west pavilion added by Thomas Jefferson.

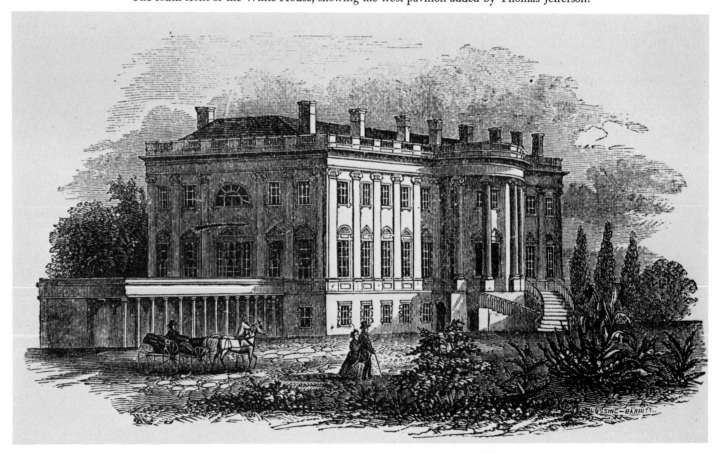

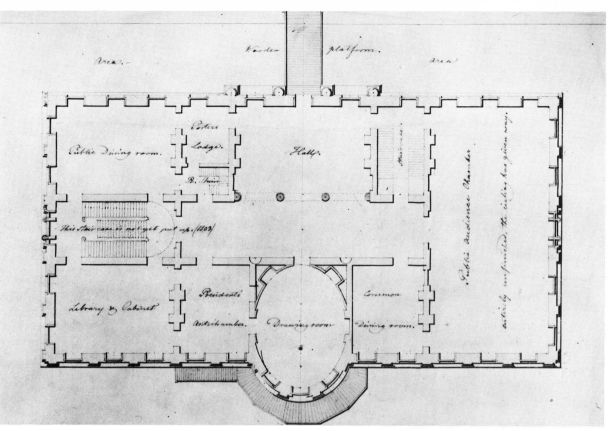

"Plan of the Principal Story in 1803" of the White House, drawn by Latrobe for Jefferson in 1807, noting that the main staircase was "not yet put up," and that the "Ceiling has given way" in the public audience chamber to the east, which was "entirely unfinished."

The north front of the White House in 1801, from a drawing by W. Blodgett.

The Blue Room in 1889, with decoration by Louis C. Tiffany. An early photograph by Frances Benjamin Johnston.

Model in the Smithsonian Institution of the Blue Room (before the 1814 fire). The overmantel and chairs are of Latrobe's design.

A 1974 photograph of the Blue Room. To the left of the mantel, Stuart's portrait of James Monroe.

house has uneven fenestration, as it incorporates the modest residence built in 1743 by Washington's half-brother. Although his dramatic career allowed Washington little time at Mount Vernon, he loved the place, and during his tenure managed to increase its acreage from two to eight thousand acres. The land was divided between tenanted outlying farms and the home farm attached to the house. This was mostly laid out as parkland "with the woods thinned or in clumps." The outlying farms provided the income to keep up the main house, improve the elaborate gardens and vineyard, and feed the one hundred and twenty-five slaves on the property.

George Washington married in 1759; during the preceding years he had enlarged the original house by raising it a story and connecting it to the four principal dependencies by "Pallisades." It would be interesting to know what the house, and particularly the palisades, looked like at that date. Mount Vernon took on its present aspect from 1773 onwards. Work on the house progressed slowly, on account of the War of Independence; the two-story Banquet Hall, or "New Room," begun in 1776, was still unfinished in 1784, when Lafayette was entertained there. The weathervane was finally placed on the cupola three years later. There is no record of an architect having been involved with the building in any of Washington's published writings, or in his

Edgemont, North Garden, Virginia, designed by Jefferson for his friend James Cocke in 1797. Attendant pavilions are attached to the house by underground passages.

The west façade of Edgemont.

The entrance hall of Edgemont.

Edgemont in an engraving by Milton Grigg.

domestic letters and accounts. Like his contemporary Thomas Jefferson, he designed his own improvements. One of his visitors observed, "It's astonishing with what niceness he directs everything in the building way, condescending even to measure the things himself, that all may be perfectly uniform."

The house is faced with "rusticated Boards," sanded to resemble stone. The portico facing the river was added in 1784, and later surmounted by the Chinese balustrade, so familiar from illustrations of Mount Vernon on everything from grandfather clocks to cups and saucers. This balustrade was in place in 1858, but it has not been restored, and the river front is the poorer without it.

In spite of the crowds of visitors, the house has a comfortable atmosphere, and the interior has been most sensitively cared for. It has not been over-restored, and as a result still retains the faded charm and character of a country house. Some of the woodcarving is exceptionally fine, and the mantel in the Banquet Hall, sent by an English admirer named Samuel Vaughan, was even rather too grand for Washington's taste. In thanking the donor for it, he wrote: "I have the honour to inform you that the chimney-piece is arrived, and by the number of cases (ten) too elegant and costly by far, I fear for my own room, and republican stile of living."

This elaborate mantel, carved in Italy, provided the motifs that are found in the Adamesque plaster ceiling executed by a Mr. Rawlins in 1786. Washington, uncertain about the finishing of the room, asked in a letter to his friend Vaughan if the stuccowork should be painted "or are they left of the natural colour given by the cement made according to Mr. Higgin's mode of preparing it? And also, whether the rooms thus finished are stuccoed below the surbase (chair high) or from thence upwards only?" It does seem curious that it is not *Mrs.* Washington who takes up the pen to Clement Biddle in Philadelphia, January 17, 1784: "I have seen rooms with gilded borders; made, I believe, of papier Maché fastnd with Brads or Cement around the Doors and window Casings, Surbase & ca.; and which gives a plain blew, or green paper a rich and handsome look. Is there any to be had in Philadelpa?, and at what price? Is there any plain blew or green Paper to be had also? the price (by the yard and width)." Again an echo of Jefferson. Mrs. Jefferson died young, but had she lived it is hard to imagine her husband leaving decisions of this nature to her.

Wye House, Talbot County, Maryland, was completed in 1784 for Edward Lloyd IV, to replace an earlier house destroyed by fire. The identity of the architect is not known. It was originally built in three separate parts, and subsequently the flankers were joined to the central block by hyphens containing small rooms and passages. Further additions at either end completed a seven-part composition paralleled, in Maryland, only at Whitehall. Wye House is a rural version of the Hammond–Harwood house, which the Lloyds had watched being built across the street from their Annapolis residence, where Mary Tayloe Lloyd, Edward Lloyd's daughter, was married to Francis Scott Key, writer of "The Star Spangled Banner."

Mrs. Lloyd was born Elizabeth Tayloe of Mount Airy, and it may have been for her that an existing glasshouse at Wye was enlarged into the architectural orangery, somewhat grander than

151

Blennerhassett Island, Parkersburg, West Virginia, built by Harman Blennerhassett and finished c. 1799, on an island in the Ohio River. Aaron Burr came here after his duel with Alexander Hamilton, to plot with Blennerhassett the formation of an empire in the southwest. The house, which was built of wood, had a façade of 110 feet and must have been the equal in scale of the grandest mansions on the eastern seaboard.

the one at her home. It balances the house at the end of the bowling green, where peacocks strut back and forth. The family has been seated here since 1623, and the house is still the focus of a working plantation.

Hampton, Baltimore County, Maryland, was built for Charles and Rebecca Ridgely in 1783. Research in the complete set of family records deposited with the Maryland Historical Society by Mr. and Mrs. John Ridgely, the last occupants of the house, has failed to reveal the architect. The only name mentioned is that of John Howell, carpenter, who was paid the large sum of £3482 for his work. When Howell died in 1787, he was described in a Baltimore newspaper as "a very ingenious architect." He may have been just a skilled overseer, which could account for the highly unusual design of the house.

The cupola (or "doom," as it appears in the carpenter's accounts) is an uncommon feature in a grand house of the date of Hampton. Such adornments were popular with Wren and his followers, and again in the Victorian period, but surprising to find in 1783. Strangest of all are the two porticoes to front and back. If, as appears to be the case, they have never been altered, they are unique. The pediments, which contain a miniature Palladian window with a Gibbs surround, are supported by giant square columns joined to respondent pilasters by screen walls. Three urns decorate them and add to the effect; more urns are scattered around the cupola and at the base of the roof. Hampton is indeed an interesting house, and one of its size must surely have elicited comments of some kind in its day. A fuller picture is bound to emerge in time.

The interior is more conventional; a great hall stretches from front to back, with reception rooms opening off it. The best feature of the house is the bedroom landing, which has eight *rétardataire* doorcases with broken pediments, four of them dummy, and a Greek frieze.

The Ridgelys were prosperous landowners and merchants, but it was the discovery of iron on land that they owned, and the establishment of a furnace, that enabled them to build a house on such a large scale. It remained in the family until 1948. In that year it was acquired by the Avalon Foundation and presented to the Federal Government. The Foundation made funds available for its restoration, and Hampton is now open to the public under the auspices of the Society for the Preservation of Maryland Antiquities.

Peter Lacour's drawing of the Federal Hall, on Wall Street in the City of New York, shows the inauguration of George Washington as first President of the United States, which took place there on April 30, 1789. The engraving by Amos Doolittle was published in the following year. The building, which incorporated part of the old City Hall (1699), was designed in 1788 by Pierre L'Enfant. The acclaim accorded it no doubt helped to secure for L'Enfant the task of laying out the new capital city to be built on the banks of the Potomac. The Senate Chamber, immediately behind the balcony on the piano nobile, is described in the *Massachusetts Magazine: or Monthly Museum of Knowledge and Rational Entertainment*, for June 1789 as follows:

> The Senate Chamber is decorated with pilasters, etc. which are not of any regular order; the proportions are light and graceful; the capitals are of a fanciful kind, the invention of Major L'Enfant, the architect; he has appropriated them to this building, for amidst their

Semple House, Williamsburg, Virginia. The gable ends form pediments.

foliage appears a star and rays, and a piece of drapery below suspends a small medallion with U.S. in a cypher. The idea is new and the effect pleasing; and although they cannot be said to be of any ancient order, we must allow that they have an appearance of magnificence. The ceiling is plain with only a sun and thirteen stars in the center. The marble which is used in the chimnies is American, and the beauty of shades and polish is equal to any of its kind in Europe. The President's chair is at one end of the room, elevated about three feet from the floor, under a rich canopy of crimson damask.

The Representatives' room, the actual Federal Hall, was at the back of the building on the ground floor. There were two galleries for the public, one above the other, and the great chamber was octagonal, enabling the maximum use to be made of the site at one end, and providing support for the galleries at the other. The room was sixty feet long and thirty high, decorated with "trophies, and other emblematical fancy figures, together with the arms of the United States . . . and the letters U. S. in a cypher, surrounded with laurel. The Speaker's chair is opposite the great door and raised by several steps; the chairs for the members are ranged semicircularly in two rows in front of the speaker. . . . It is intended to place a statue of Liberty over the speaker's chair. . . ."

National emblems were also used to adorn the exterior of Federal Hall, to render it properly a "building set apart for national purposes." "The frieze is ingeniously divided to admit thirteen stars in the metopes; these, with the American Eagle and other insignia in the pediment, in the tablets over the windows, filled with the thirteen arrows and the olive branch united. . . ."

The national and historical associations of Federal Hall did not suffice to save it from destruction, and in 1812 it was pulled down, during the lifetime of its creator L'Enfant.

A competition was held in 1792 for the building of a "President's Palace" in Washington, to be ready for occupancy when the capital moved from Philadelphia to a district "not exceeding 10 miles sq" on the Potomac River. In the words of Pierre L'Enfant it was to have "the sumptuousness of a palace and the agreeableness of [a] country seat." Thomas Jefferson, under the pseudonym AZ, entered a drawing that was a version of the Rotonda. Had it been chosen, he would, when elected third President in 1801, have enjoyed the unusual privilege of moving into an official residence of which he was himself the architect.

James Hoban, an Irish architect who had migrated to America to build "houses for gentlemen," succeeded in winning the competition. His design is borrowed from Leinster House, which in turn is derived from Castletown; Castletown may therefore claim to be the grandfather of the White House. All three have a plan with axial corridors running from east to west. The familiar entrance portico was added to the imposing but conventional block in 1829, and the circular portico on the garden front to the south is five years earlier.

Mrs. John Adams, the first First Lady to occupy the White House, was far from happy with it. She wrote in 1800:

The house is upon a grand and superb scale, requiring about thirty servants to attend and keep the apartments in proper order, and perform the ordinary business of the house and stables; and established very well proportioned to the President's salary. The lighting . . . is a tax indeed; and the fires we are obliged to keep, to secure us from daily agues, is another very cheering comfort. To assist us in this great castle . . . bells are wholly wanting . . . surrounded with forests, wood is not to be had, because people can not be found to cut it and cart it. . . . You must keep this to yourself, and when asked how I like it, say I write you the situation is beautiful, which is true. The house is made habitable, but there is not a single apartment finished . . . the great unfinished audience room I make a drying room of. . . . The principal stairs are not up, and will not be this Winter.

Although generously concluding that "It is a beautiful spot, capable of every improvement, and the more I view it, the more I am delighted with it," she was unable to resist the tart observation that "If the twelve years, in which this place has been considered as the future seat of government, had

The Sally Billie House, Halifax County, North Carolina, a small adaptation of the Semple House form.

Lilac Hill, Howard County, Missouri, built c. 1830, a derivative of the Semple House.

Madewood Plantation, Bayou Lafourche, Louisiana, built in 1844, at the height of the Greek Revival, is a grander version of the Hazel-Nash House.

Hazel-Nash House, Hillsborough, North Carolina. Three pediments face the front.

Brett Doll House, made in New York City in 1830 in the familiar three-part pattern.

Hayes Plantation, Edenton, North Carolina. The façade has curved sweeps with double columns and contains a Gothic library in one wing. The house was built c. 1818.

A vaulted corridor in Bremo.

The west front of Bremo.

Bremo, Bremo Bluffs, Virginia, was built in 1818 by John Neilson, an architect who had worked with Jefferson and Cocke at the University of Virginia.

Temple in the Bremo garden.

been improved, as they would have been if in New England, very many of the inconveniences would have been removed." Thomas Jefferson, Adams's successor in office, described the house as "big enough for two emperors, one Pope, and the Grand Lama." He suggested both porticoes and added the colonnades to either side which conceal rooms for fuel, stores, and garden sheds; "offices" in the old sense of the word; today they are offices in the modern sense. The disposition of kitchens, workshops, and the like at Monticello was not dissimilar.

In 1814, British troops set fire to the Capitol and the President's House. Hoban was called in to rebuild, and it was decided to hide the cracks in the walls by painting the house white; it has remained the White House ever since. In July of 1818, Robert Donaldson, recently graduated from the University of North Carolina, paid a visit to the residence, then still in the process of restoration. He reported in his journal that "the President was now at his country seat—& Workmen were employed in finishing and re-papering the House—The Foreman kindly conducted us through the House and explained everything . . . we entered a Saloon which is Elyptical—crimson papering, with rich Gilt bordering,—the windows and cornices with large gilded, spread Eagles. This Room is decorated with a full length portrait (by Trumbull) [sic] of Washington at his Bureau,—with volumes of the Revolution & Constitution by him. This is the most splendid Room."

Succeeding Presidents have modified the interior according to the fashion of the day, and the guidebook contains old photographs showing how it has changed over the years. It progressed from Greek to "steamboat" to *art nouveau* to neo-Restoration, with dark paneling and pseudo-

Borough House, Stateburg, South Carolina, built in 1758. Dr. William Wallace Anderson, whose wife had inherited the property, added the portico and wings in 1821.

Carolean plasterwork, in 1902. In 1952 the structure was reckoned unsafe, and the building was gutted once more. It was put back in "Officers' Mess Georgian," and although the interior will be altered, the White House will probably remain unchanged architecturally for many years to come.

The plan of the Villa Rotonda evidently fascinated Thomas Jefferson. His entry for the President's Palace competition was a version of it, and so was a design he made for the Governor's mansion at Richmond, although neither of these was built. Poplar Forest, a house he built in the shape of an octagon, fits into this category also. It is at Edgemont, North Garden, Virginia, designed by Jefferson for his friend James Cocke, that the Palladian spirit finds its purest expression. The house has a portico for every cardinal point, and is the epitome of everything that was most admired of Palladio in the New World, combining as it does simplicity with elegance, and beauty with convenience. A fuller description of both houses will be found in *Mr. Jefferson, Architect*, by Guinness and Sadler.

Palladian houses both large and small are to be found in every part of the United States. One of the most "correct" of the smaller examples is the Semple House in Williamsburg, which is a remarkably perfect composition seen from any angle. The projections on either side end in pediments following the line of the roof, a most ingenious solution skillfully handled. Built before 1782, its design has been attributed, on slender evidence, to Thomas Jefferson.

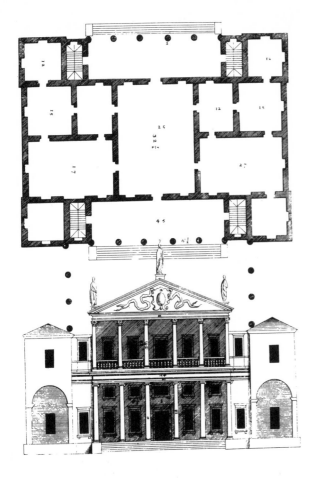

Villa Valmarana, Lisiera, near Vicenza, taken from Palladio's *Quattro Libri*, Book II, Plate 42. In his description: "This fabric has two courts; one forward, for the use of the master, and the other backward, where the corn is threshed: and has covertures, in which are accommodated all the places belonging to the use of a villa."

The Sally Billie House in Halifax County, North Carolina (c. 1800), is a derivative of the Semple House plan, smaller and less sophisticated than the original; it contains a Chinese Chippendale staircase of miniature proportions. At the time of writing, the house is being restored as an example of this particular adaptation, found only in the United States, of the Palladian villa. Lilac Hill, Howard County, Missouri, built thirty years later, is a brick house on the same plan, with a naïve Palladian window in the pediment. The design is not so ingenious as the Semple House, however, and the sides of the building are by no means so well finished, although there is the hint of a pediment.

The Hazel–Nash House, Hillsboro, North Carolina, is yet another version. A single pediment crowns the central block, which is flanked by matching wings; each of the three pediments has a Gothic window to scale. The design is taken from Morris's *Select Architecture*, and the addition of a large porch is a concession to the climate. Another tripartite arrangement is that found at Madewood, a more elaborate version of the Hazel–Nash house, where the size of the pedimented frontispiece is accentuated by the proximity of the wings, close beside the main body of the house. Madewood, near New Orleans on Bayou Lafourche, was built in 1844 by Henry Howard for the Pugh family, and is open to the public.

The Brett doll's house was made in 1830 for the New York family of that name, and the outline is again that of a Palladian villa, filtered down through pattern books to a carpentry shop and thence to the nursery of some fortunate child. Ask a child to draw a house, and the result is likely to be a rendering of the balanced Palladian scheme.

162

The Pavilion (1825), Ticonderoga, New York, in an 1828 lithograph.

The lake front of The Pavilion.

One of the flanking galleries of The Pavilion, originally an open porch, with a sofa by Duncan Phyfe.

The entrance hall of The Pavilion, with chandelier from Otsego Hall, the Cooperstown home of James Fenimore Cooper.

Fiske Kimball, the Jefferson scholar, wrote in 1949: "Of all the houses in the Jeffersonian tradition, not even excepting Monticello, it is Bremo which makes the deepest impression of artistic perfection. Monticello we see drastically remodeled by Jefferson after a change of conception. Bremo has the inevitability of a single ordered creation. Calm, monumental and serene, it commands our emotion as a masterpiece of the art of form." Although the cornerstone, laid in July 1818, clearly states "John Neilson of Albemarle Architect," it was widely believed for many years that Bremo was designed by Thomas Jefferson. Architect and builder were somewhat interchangeable

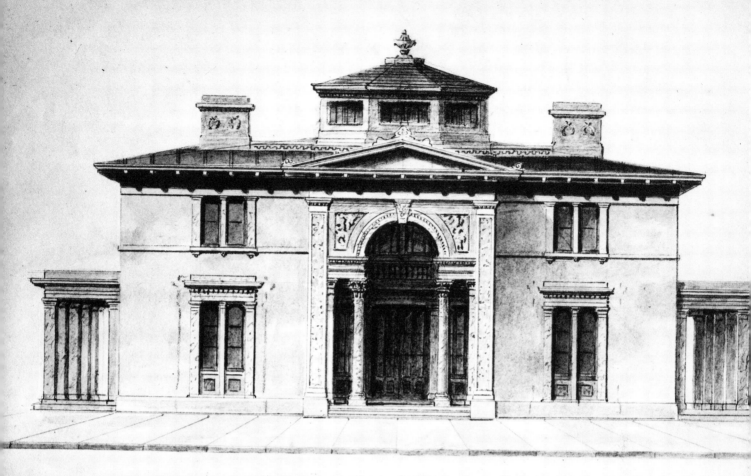

PALMYREAN?

TUSCAN CORNICE   ROMAN   PALLADIA

Drawing by A. J. Davis, better known for his Gothic essays.

appellations at that time. Later evidence indicates that the house was in fact designed and built by Neilson, working closely with the owner, General John Hartwell Cocke.

General Cocke did indeed ask Jefferson's advice when he determined to build Bremo; Colonel Isaac Coles wrote to Cocke (February 23, 1816): "With Mr. Jefferson I conversed at length on the subject of architecture. Palladio, he said, 'was the Bible.' You should get it and stick close to it. He had sent all books, etc. to Washington or he would have drawn up yr. House for you —it would have been a pleasure to him." Neilson and James Dinsmore, "superior house joiners" who had worked at Monticello and Montpelier, came to see the General at Bremo Recess. Dinsmore was by that time fully occupied at the University of Virginia, and full credit for the design must go to Neilson.

Bremo stands on the crest of a hill overlooking the valley of the James. The central block with three Tuscan porticoes contains the principal rooms on two floors. The pavilions contain the schoolroom and kitchen; other services are in the links and in separate buildings nearby. At the north end of the lower lawn there is a group of farm buildings beside a splendid Palladian barn, built in 1815. Two of these outbuildings are made of pisé de terre, which is made by tamping down a wet mix of clay, lime, and pebbles, layer after layer, in wooden forms. When this mixture has dried, it much resembles adobe in toughness, and, properly stuccoed to keep out the weather, will stand for centuries.

A small classical temple dedicated to the Sons of Temperance stands at the southern end of the lower lawn. General Cocke was president of the United States Temperance Society and originally raised the temple over a spring on the canal bank, so that passing boatmen could refresh themselves with a dipper of cool water rather than swig from a rum cask. The General was also opposed to the use of tobacco, and it was a crop that he refused to grow. The design of this little building seems to have been adapted from a drawing sent to Cocke by the New York architect A. J. Davis in August 1847. Davis was then building Belmead, the first of the James River Gothic mansions, on the river between Bremo and Richmond, a commission he had received from the General's son, Philip St. George Cocke.

There is a curious interplay of architectural styles between the Cocke plantations. Having completed his great house in the classical tradition, in 1844 General Cocke remodeled the older family home, Bremo Recess, into a Gothic folly with pointed arches, curved and stepped gables, and clustered chimneys. Philip, on the other hand, built a simple, somewhat naïve version of the great Palladian stone barn at Bremo, but elected the most modish of Gothic designs for his country villa.

Province House, Prince Edward Island, Canada, designed by Isaac Smith in 1843, was the principal administrative building for the province. Colonial statesmen met here in 1864 to lay the plans that led to the Confederation. It is one of many official buildings in Canada to demonstrate "an architectural show of political power." The design was perhaps taken from the east wing of Osgood Hall, Toronto (1829).

Hedworth House (1717), Durham, England. The plan and elevation from Campbell's *Vitruvius Britannicus*.

Fifteen miles below Camden, South Carolina, all that remains of the town of Stateburg lies along the old mail-coach road from Charleston. Stateburg was established in 1783 by a group of neighboring landowners who hoped to make it the state capital. A courthouse, jail, post office, academy, library, and tavern were erected in rapid succession by the optimistic planners, but despite their efforts the honors went to Columbia. Two churches and a scattering of old houses along the High Hills of the Santee are all that survive today of an ambitious dream.

The oldest of these remaining houses is thought to be Borough House, first known as Hill-crest, which has a frame central section dating from 1758. During the Revolutionary War it was occupied for a period by General Cornwallis, and later, when the tide of conflict had turned, served as headquarters for General Nathanael Greene of the Continental Army. It was owned at that time by Thomas Hooper, whose brother was one of the North Carolina signers of the Declaration of Independence. The Hoopers bequeathed Borough House to a niece, the wife of Dr. William Wallace Anderson of Maryland, and it is still in the possession of their descendants.

The Andersons did much to beautify the grounds, and in 1821 tore down the original clapboard wings on either side and replaced them in pisé; Dr. Anderson was one of several plantation owners who were at that time experimenting with this novel building material. He also erected five pisé outbuildings, including the library, kitchen, schoolhouse, and his little temple-form medical office at the north gates.

The whole house, frame and pisé alike, has been stuccoed to give it a unified appearance. The two-tiered portico, with plain Ionic columns turned from the heartwood of long-leaf pine like those on the library and office, faces the entrance drive. There are full entablatures above each tier of columns, those of the upper story resting on pedestals linked by classical balustrades. At the center of the west front there are six Ionic pilasters on the upper story, and a three-bay loggia at ground level, recalling Palladio's Villa Valmarana at Lisiera. This front looks over the pre-Revolutionary garden to the Santee River valley beyond. An early conservatory at the south end of the house is a reminder of the family interest in botany. Dr. Anderson counted among his horticultural friends the Hon. Joel Poinsett, who died while visiting Borough House in 1851, and lies buried in the graveyard of the nearby Church of the Holy Cross.

Dr. Anderson, like General Cocke, further satisfied his love of building by remodeling a neighboring plantation house, The Oaks, in 1832, for the benefit of his relatives Jolly and Merry Bracey. The building is an ingenious architectural exercise and resembles a simple version in clapboard of Borough House.

Clarendon Court, Newport, Rhode Island, built in 1904 by Horace Trumbauer for
Edward Knight, the elevation being taken from Campbell's Hedworth design.

In the seventeenth century the Pells were granted a large tract of land in Westchester
County, New York, but the Revolution found them in the Loyalist camp, and the manor was con-
fiscated. William Ferris Pell, deprived of his inheritance, founded a New York City firm that
imported mahogany and Italian marble. His business took him frequently to the then flourishing
town of Burlington, Vermont, on Lake Champlain, and while traveling up the lake in 1808, Pell
was much taken with the great star-shaped ruin of Fort Ticonderoga. He determined to acquire
the promontory on which it stands, and in 1820 completed its purchase from Columbia and Union
colleges, joint title-holders. He at once took steps to fence the fort and put a stop to its being used
as a quarry. In saving the ruin from further depredation, he initiated the earliest program of historic
restoration in the State of New York. Subsequent generations of Pells have continued his work,
and the Vaubanesque fort is now restored and open to visitors in summer. It was built by the
French as a southern outpost in 1755 and had a momentous history of siege and capture up to the
Revolution. No longer of strategic importance, it was left to decay, and by the time William Pell
caught sight of it, the fort had become a picturesque ruin.

Pell built The Pavilion about a quarter of a mile from the old bastion in 1826, to a design
of his own invention. The ramparts of the fort can be seen across the formal garden at the back of
the house, closing the view inland. Not long before, in 1768, the great ruin at Fountains Abbey
had been brought in as a climax to a landscape garden in Yorkshire. The formal garden at the
Pavilion was laid out by a French officer in 1757, and walled in by Stephen Pell in 1908.

The Pavilion is among the earliest houses built as a refuge from the summer heat of New
York City, and a steamboat began to ply the lake in 1808, which made the point more accessible.
William Pell numbered among his customers the outstanding cabinetmaker of the period in New
York, Duncan Phyfe. There are a great many Phyfe pieces still in the house, and there may have

been an element of barter in their acquisition. Their clean lines match the uncluttered simplicity of the interior, which has been arranged by Mrs. Henry Parrish and Albert Hadley in a most sensitive manner.

In the space of a few minutes the visitor who drives down Belleview Avenue in Newport is exposed to a bewildering architectural panoply. One after another the "cottages" represent a variety of styles and reflect the cultures of many countries, standing side by side in startling juxta-position. They were built in the Victorian and Edwardian eras when Newport was *the* resort for persons of great wealth, and renowned, as it is today, as a yachting center. Gone was the puritan modesty that had kept domestic architecture in check. The Newport cottages vie with one another in splendid vulgarity, each trying to outdo its neighbor.

There is one modest and dignified exception to this rule, Clarendon Court, built in 1904 by Horace Trumbauer for Edward Knight, a retired railroad executive from Pennsylvania. An eclectic architect, Trumbauer also designed The Elms and Miramar in the French taste, but here it was to England that he turned for inspiration. He took the elevation from Plate 88 in Campbell's *Vitruvius Britannicus*, a house Campbell had designed in 1717 for John Hedworth, Esq., M. P., in Chester-le-Street, Durham. The English counterpart of Clarendon Court was pulled down at just the same time as its model came to life in the New World. The American version adheres faithfully to Campbell's design except for the cupolas over the wings, which Trumbauer omitted, and the floor plan, which was not followed. It is a chaste essay in Anglo-Palladian taste, somewhat out of place among the monstrous giants of Newport.

Wethersfield House, Dutchess County, New York. The *glorietta,* added in 1973, was designed by George Frederick Poehler, and is frescoed by Annigoni.

Rose Hall, Jamaica, British West Indies, c. 1775.

"Were a modern architect to build a palace in Lapland, or the West Indies, Palladio would be his guide, nor would he dare to stir a step without his book."

—William Hogarth

THE WEST INDIES

The hostile climate of New England and a puritan dislike of ostentation combined to discourage the building of lavish houses in the continental Colonies. There was no such restraint among the planters in the Caribbean, and the period of prosperity that ended with the Free Trade Act of 1846 gave rise to a splendid architectural heritage. Rose Hall (c. 1775), Jamaica, exceeds in size any private house of its day in the New World. It has recently been restored under the supervision of the late T. A. L. Concannon, and it is hoped that funds will be forthcoming to re-erect the curved quadrants and wings, the foundations of which remain.

The little Counting House at Good Hope Plantation, Falmouth, is only one of several Palladian buildings to survive. Marlborough Great House (1793), near Mandeville, is an example of good architectural manners, with mahogany columns painted white, and stands high, affording spectacular views, as do Rose Hall and Good Hope.

The Governor of Jamaica lived in a vast seventeen-bay palace known as King's House, taking up the whole of the west side of King's Square in Spanish Town. The former House of Assembly faces it across the square, the Courts of Justice are on the south side, and on the north a curved arcade centers on a domed octagon surmounted by a balustrade and a cupola. This contains the Rodney Memorial, and was erected in 1785 to commemorate his victory at the Battle of the Saints in 1782. The architect is unknown, but the life-size statue of the Admiral was sent over from England and is the work of John Bacon.

Nassau has less dramatic buildings and none of the mountainous beauty of Jamaica, but the town has a faded colonial charm. The houses stand close together, bougainvillea tumbling over their walls, verandas tightly shuttered against the glare of the sun. The town is dominated by the

Counting House, Good Hope Plantation,
Falmouth, Jamaica, 1755.

Malborough Great House, Jamaica, built in
1793. The designer may have been the
Scottish architect Forsyth.

The Rodney Memorial, Spanish Town, Jamaica, forms one side of King's Square. The statue of Admiral Lord Rodney by John Bacon (1740–1799) stands beneath the dome.

La Feuillie, Lyford Cay, New Providence, Bahamas. A Roman "ruin" built in 1964, it shines like a jewel among its neighbors.

The triumphal arch and rusticated wall of La Feuillie shield the garden from the sea.

Heron Bay, Barbados, 1947. The entrance front.

The Heron Bay drawing room walls are of coquina.

gleaming white portico of Government House, under which the band marches to and fro each morning, playing martial music. Lower down, a miniature square has handsome symmetrical buildings with porticoes facing a statue of Queen Victoria. The buildings in Nassau are plastered and painted either white, plum, or Roman apricot. Unfortunately, the prosperity which has invaded the town is beginning to prove its undoing. Banks and blocks of flats are creeping up on the mysterious old houses, and if this trend is allowed to continue, the character of the town will be destroyed.

At Lyford Cay, on the far side of the island, a Palladian folly has been built by the actress and writer Rosanna Seaborn, who is at present preparing a film script on the Canadian Rebellion of 1837. The architect was A. F. Robjohns, and building commenced in 1964. An oval pool, surrounded by coral stone, is screened from the sea by a rusticated wall with round-headed windows to either side of a triumphal arch. If there is a stone missing here and there at La Feuillie, or a piece seems to have fallen off the parapet, this is to convey the effect of a ruin, stumbled upon in some Roman settlement in North Africa.

A tradition of classical stone-built houses goes back further on Barbados than on the American mainland. Coral stone was as plentiful as the labor necessary for working it, timber was scarce and expensive, and, on an island prone to hurricanes, stone buildings lend a sense of security.

The sea aspect of Heron Bay.

The garden court of Heron Bay.

Heron Bay, Barbados, was built in 1947 by Mr. and Mrs. Ronald Tree and their architect, Geoffrey Jellicoe. It is a variant of the design of the Villa Maser with which this book begins, and therefore makes a suitable ending. Built of the local coral stone, a dominant portico at the center, the arcaded arms that at Maser are straight here curve forward to meet the sea. The garden courtyard thus created is filled with the brilliant color of tropical flowers and trees.

The climate in the Islands is not unlike an Italian summer all year round, and the garden court of Heron Bay with its carpet of flowers has become the main living room of the house. The arcades enfolding it form a curving passage lit by tall arches. In a climate where tropical rains are apt to descend virtually without warning, this arcade provides welcome cover. At the top of the steps behind the great portico is the drawing room on the piano nobile. A double cube with walls of natural coral stone, it is a room where Palladio should have felt at home. From it can be seen the white sandy beach, and beyond, the green of the turquoise sea turning gradually to blue as it goes out to meet the sky.

OVERLEAF: Dusk, Heron Bay.

177

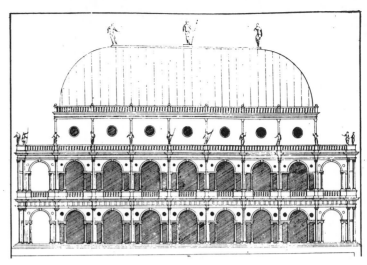

The Basilica at Vicenza: "... the portico's it has round it are of my invention ..."

Selected Bibliography

Ackerman, James S. *Palladio*. Baltimore: Penguin Books, Inc., 1967.

Antiques Magazine, XCVII (April, 1970), *passim*.

Beirne, Rosamond Randall, and Scarff, John Henry. *William Buckland, Architect of Virginia and Maryland*. Privately printed: Board of Regents, Gunston Hall and Hammond-Harwood House Association, 1970.

Bridenbaugh, Carl. *Peter Harrison, First American Architect*. Chapel Hill: The University of North Carolina Press, 1949. London: Oxford University Press, 1949.

Campbell, Colen. *Vitruvius Britannicus: or the British Architect.*, Vols. I, II, and III. London: M.DCC.-XXXI.

Chamberlain, Samuel and Narcissa. *Southern Interiors*. New York: Hastings House, 1956.

Chastellux, Marquis de. *Travels in North America in the Years 1780, 1781, and 1782*, Vols. I and II. Tr. by Howard C. Rice, Jr. Williamsburg: Institute of Early American History and Culture—University of North Carolina Press, 1963.

Downing, Antoinette Forrester, and Scully, Vincent Joseph, Jr. *The Architectural Heritage of Newport, Rhode Island, 1640–1915*. Cambridge: Harvard University Press, 1952.

Fletcher, Bannister F. *Andrea Palladio*. London: George Bell and Sons, 1902.

Great Houses of Italy. Ed. by the Editors of *Réalités*. New York, G. P. Putnam's Sons, 1968.

Guinness, Desmond. *Portrait of Dublin*. New York: The Viking Press, 1967. London: Batsford, 1967.

Guinness, Desmond, and Ryan, William. *Irish Houses and Castles*. London: Thames and Hudson, 1971. New York: The Viking Press, 1971.

Guinness, Desmond, and Sadler, Julius Trousdale, Jr. *Mr. Jefferson, Architect*. New York: The Viking Press, 1973.

Hussey, Christopher. *English Country Houses: Early Georgian*. London: Country Life Ltd., 1955.

———. *English Gardens and Landscapes, 1700–1750*. New York: Funk & Wagnalls, 1967: London: Country Life Ltd., 1967.

Jacobs, Flora Gill. *A History of Dolls' Houses*. New York: Charles Scribner's Sons, 1965.

Johnston, Francis Benjamin, and Waterman, Thomas Tileston. *The Early Architecture of North Carolina*. Chapel Hill: The University of North Carolina Press, 1947.

Kent, William. *The Designs of Inigo Jones*. Vols. I and II. London: M.DCC.XXVII.

Kimball, Fiske. *Mr. Samuel McIntire, Carver: The Architect of Salem*. Portland: The Southworth-Anthoensen Press, 1940.

———. *Thomas Jefferson, Architect*. New York: Da Capo Press, 1968.

Kirker, Harold. *The Architecture of Charles Bulfinch*. Cambridge: Harvard University Press, 1969.

Lees-Milne, James. *Earls of Creation*. New York: London House & Maxwell, 1963.

Leiding, Harriette Kershaw. *Historic Houses of South Carolina*. Philadelphia and London: J. B. Lippincott Company, 1921.

Levey, Michael. *The Later Italian Pictures in the*

Collection of Her Majesty the Queen. London: The Phaidon Press, 1964. New York: New York Graphic Society, 1964.

Loth, Calder, and Sadler, Julius Trousdale, Jr. *The Only Proper Style: Gothic Architecture in the United States.* Boston: New York Graphic Society, Ltd., 1975.

Mazzotti, Giuseppe. *Palladian and Other Venetian Villas.* Rome: Carlo Bestetti, Edizioni D'Arte, 1966.

Nichols, Frederick Doveton. *Thomas Jefferson's Architectural Drawings.* Charlottesville: University of Virginia Press, 1961.

O'Neal, William B. *Architecture in Virginia.* New York: Walker & Co., 1968.

Palladio, Andrea. *The Four Books of Architecture.* Tr. by Isaac Ware. London: R. Ware, n.d.

Puppi, Lionello. *Andrea Palladio.* Vols. I and II. Milano: Electra Editrice, 1973.

————. *Andrea Palladio,* Boston: New York Graphic Society, 1975.

Ravenal, Beatrice St. Julien. *Architects of Charleston.* Charleston: Carolina Art Association, 1945.

Reif, Rita. *Treasure Rooms of American Mansions, Manors, and Houses.* New York: Coward, McCann, & Geoghegan, Inc., 1970.

Reynolds, James. *Andrea Palladio and the Winged Device.* New York: Creative Age Press, 1948.

Roop, Guy. *Villas and Palaces of Andrea Palladio.* Milano: Arti Grafiche Francesco Ghezzi, MCMLXVII.

Senenzato, Camillo. *The Rotonda of Andrea Palladio.* University Park and London: The Pennsylvania State University Press, 1968.

Sitwell, Sacheverell. *Great Houses of Europe.* New York: G. P. Putnam's Sons, 1961.

Smith, Alice R. Huger and D. E. Huger. *The Dwelling Houses of Charleston, South Carolina.* Philadelphia and London: J. B. Lippincott Company, 1917.

Stoney, Samuel Gaillard. *Plantations of the Carolina Low Country.* 3rd ed. Charleston: The Carolina Art Association, 1945.

Stutchbury, Howard E. *The Architecture of Colen Campbell.* Cambridge: Harvard University Press, 1967. Manchester: Manchester University Press, 1967.

Summerson, John. *Architecture in Britain, 1530–1830.* London: Penguin Publishing Company, Ltd., 1963. 4th edition, rev. and enlarged.

———— *Inigo Jones.* Hammondsworth, England: Penguin Books, Ltd., 1966.

Tinkcom, Margaret. "Cliveden: the Building of a Philadelphia Countryseat, 1763–1767," *Pennsylvania Magazine of History and Biography,* Vol. LXXXVIII, No. 1, January 1964.

Tipping, H. Avray. *English Homes. Period V—Vol. I. Early Georgian, 1714–1760.* London: Country Life Ltd., MCMXXI.

Vitruvius. *The Ten Books of Architecture.* Tr. by Morris Hicky Morgan. New York: Dover Publications, Inc., 1960.

Waterman, Thomas Tileston. *The Mansions of Virginia, 1706–1776.* Chapel Hill: The University of North Carolina Press, 1947.

Whiffen, Marcus. *The Eighteenth-Century Houses of Williamsburg.* Williamburg, Virginia: Colonial Williamsburg, 1960.

Wittkower, Rudolph. *Palladio and English Palladianism.* London: Thames and Hudson, 1974. New York: George Braziller, Inc., 1974.

Index

Page numbers in italics indicate illustrations.